Religious Education in a Pluralistic Society

Papers from a Consultation on Theology and Education
held at Westhill College, Selly Oak
(an Affiliated College of the University of Birmingham)

Edited by M. C. Felderhof

HODDER AND STOUGHTON
LONDON SYDNEY AUCKLAND TORONTO

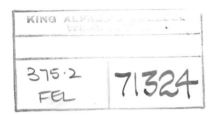
British Library Cataloguing in Publication Data

Religious education in a pluralistic society: papers
from a consultation on theology and education
held at Westhill College, Selly Oak (an affiliated
college of the University of Birmingham).
1. Religious education——Great Britain
I. Felderhof, M.C.
200'.7'1041   BV1470.G7
ISBN 0-340-35413-5

First published 1985

Printed and bound in Great Britain for
Hodder and Stoughton Educational,
a division of Hodder and Stoughton Ltd,
Mill Road, Dunton Green, Sevenoaks, Kent,
by Page Bros (Norwich) Ltd.

Contents

Foreword

Alan G. Bamford

Westhill College has a special interest in the academic disciplines represented by the papers in this book. Our major concern is the development and education of children and young people and to this end we train teachers and youth leaders to work in education, in schools and in society at large. Our motivation for this task is grounded in the Christian traditions represented by the Free Churches and was made possible through the generous support and encouragement of the Cadbury family. Today, the college is one of Britain's Institutions of Higher Education and affiliated to the University of Birmingham. It is also one of the founder members of the Selly Oak Colleges Federation which is known worldwide for its services to education, Christian mission and inter-faith studies and dialogue.

On the occasion of the seventy-fifth anniversary of the college's foundation we thought it appropriate to bring together theological and educational concerns in a major consultation. These were focused in particular on the growing pluralism of our society, of which Birmingham, where we are located, is a most poignant example. Through our international student body and academic contacts we were conscious that the questions posed were by no means solely of interest to scholars in Britain. They were also pressing issues abroad. With this in mind academics and religious leaders from different world faiths, who come from diverse national and cultural backgrounds were invited to share their perspectives and learn from each other. This had a most encouraging response and the outcome was a very stimulating and fruitful dialogue. The papers in this volume represent the sharpness of penetration into the issues which was continued in the discussion.

Our warmest thanks are offered to the governors of the college for their support and encouragement, the Farmington Trust for their financial assistance, and colleagues in the University Department of Theology and in the Selly Oak Colleges. A special word of appreciation must be extended to Dr W. S. Campbell, Head of the Religious and Theological

Studies Department, Mr Garth Read, Director of the Religious Education Centre, the Revd D. Tenant, Head of the Church Education Section of the College, the Bursar, and the catering and domestic staff, who all helped to organise and make possible the international consultation which led to this book.

Very special thanks are extended to Mr Marius Felderhof for his meticulous and untiring work as the Organising and Executive Secretary of this conference to make a complex operation follow through so successfully. Finally, a word of thanks must go to all the delegates who participated in the consultation and in particular to the contributors of the following papers who provided us with very substantial and refreshing stimuli for discussion.

Contributors

Alan G. Bamford is Principal of Homerton College, Cambridge (at the time of the Consultation he was Principal of Westhill College, Selly Oak, Birmingham)

M. C. Felderhof is a lecturer in Religious and Theological Studies, Teacher Education Department, Westhill College

The Right Revd *John Gibbs* was Bishop of Coventry at the time of the Consultation (retired 31 July 1985)

The Revd *Daniel W. Hardy* is a senior lecturer in the Department of Theology, University of Birmingham (from April 1986, Professor of Theology, University of Durham)

Professor *Paul H. Hirst* holds the Chair of Education in the Faculty of Education, University of Cambridge

Dr *John M. Hull* is a senior lecturer in the Faculty of Education, University of Birmingham

Dr *Ursula King* is a senior lecturer in the Department of Theology and Religious Studies, University of Leeds

Professor Dr *Johannes Lähnemann* holds a Chair in the Faculty of Education, University of Erlangen-Nürnberg

Dr *Anza A. Lema* is Associate General Secretary, Lutheran World Federation

The Revd *Howard W. Marratt* is Assistant Principal, West London Institute of Higher Education

The Very Revd Monsignor *Kevin Nichols* is a parish priest of Barnard Castle, Co. Durham

Professor Dr *Karl-Ernst Nipkow* holds a Chair jointly in the Faculty of Evangelical Theology and the Institute for Education, University of Tübingen

Professor *Stewart Sutherland* is Principal of the merged colleges: King's College, Queen Elizabeth College and Chelsea College, University of London (at the time of the Consultation he was Vice-Principal of King's College)

Professor *John H. Westerhoff* III holds the Chair of Religion and Education in the Divinity School, Duke University, North Carolina

Introduction

M. C. Felderhof

The papers in this volume were originally presented at a consultation on Theology and Education. That anyone should wish to arrange a dialogue between two such complex disciplines may itself seem surprising. The chances of speaking the same language or of having anything of interest to say to each other may appear remote. However, historically in the Western World education was a function of religious institutions and recognised to be an essential element in religious life. The existence of church schools and the foundations of universities are the inheritance of a religious interest in education, and an educational interest in religion. There must then have been a kind of dialogue between the theologian and the educator which enabled the authorities of the state to come to some agreement with the established churches about schooling in general and religious education in particular. Decisions were made about the respective authority of church and state, and the scope of their influence. Western nations, as becomes clear from the following papers, arrived at different solutions. Whatever the outcome, the decisions represented political, theological, and educational ideals and realities in interaction. Conflicts were resolved into some acceptable compromise, even if some of the inherent conceptual difficulties remained unanswered.

What brings scholars from different nations and different disciplines together at this point in time is the sense that the long standing solutions are no longer appropriate in the realities of contemporary Western life. The changed circumstances have led to common problems of a practical and theoretical nature. Two factors are readily identified: first, the decline of institutional Christianity in society has ended its domination of education. It follows that some of the 'Christian' assumptions of the educational enterprise can no longer be taken for granted. The dethronement of the church in Europe in the field of education is matched in the United States by the constitutional separation of church and state which has excluded the church from state schools. Secondly, there is a growing religious and ideological pluralism within Western society. It is the latter factor which underlines the first and which dominates the discussion.

The large influx of Muslims, Hindus, and other religious adherents into Western society, as well as the fascination for, and conversion of, the autochthonous population to other world faiths, has turned an intellectual awareness of religious pluralism into a practical reality. Ideally we should have heard more voices reflecting this, but for various reasons this was difficult to achieve. In any case, in relation to immigrants, it is the duty of the host community to open the dialogue and to explore the scope and limits of religious pluralism in an educational context. It should be realised that the encounter with *practical* pluralism is often a new experience for them as well, one which simply reinforces the threat to their identity derived from their status as a minority.

A new secular consensus might be a way of evading the problem posed by pluralism, and this may be the ultimate outcome, but for the moment the current reality of pluralism sets the agenda. As one of the outstanding philosophers of education, Professor Paul Hirst addresses himself to the problem of how education might cope with religious belief and its diversity. His analysis requires that whatever the traditions of belief might be there needs to be a common commitment to an 'open, rational, critical approach' in education. From this one position, pluralism in all other respects becomes a positive value because it may assist critical appraisal through the considerations which originate from different perspectives. If a critical spirit is nurtured in all traditions basic agreements will be possible because the physical world ensures a certain commonality in the condition of all mankind. Where a resolution of the differences cannot be achieved affirmations must be made in a spirit of humility and tolerance acknowledging the possibility that it might be otherwise.

Professor Hirst is surely right to invoke, and urge the cultivation of, the ideals of openness, rationality and a critical spirit. These are not debatable values, and there cannot be many people who wittingly espouse the obverse values. However, observation of human life reveals the need to be constantly reminded of them. If there are any reservations among theologians then these might focus on the emphasis these ideals receive to the exclusion of all other concerns. Criticism is often destructive in character and is in reality parasitic on a more constructive heritage. Rationality is sometimes too narrowly conceived; intellectual speculation with a Cartesian radical doubt as its starting point more often than not ends in a skepticism of all knowledge. Openness to a consideration of all views and possibilities of human existence may lead to a form of paralysis of uncertainty and indecision in situations where life demands a commitment. To undertake to explore an indefinite number of these possibilities is likely to prevent an appreciation of any particular one in depth. Professor Nipkow, as a theologian vitally interested in education, does not reject the critical spirit advocated by Professor Hirst but argues that in religious education this must be balanced with the need to foster roots which will give a person a 'positional identity'. The emphasis on identity is endorsed by

Professor Westerhoff from an American point of view in a different context. It is an important part of a theologian's trade to recollect the traditions and 'root-experiences' of his or her religion. When education in turn is also seen to be concerned with the transmission of culture, the theologian and educationist have common concerns, recollection being the first ingredient of transmission. Both educationist and theologian (in the past) have presumed the young belong and have the right to be incorporated into his or her culture and tradition, a presumption which is challenged by the plurality in society. The selection of what is to be recollected, together with the critical transformation of the traditions, becomes a well-nigh impossible task.

It may help to note that such selection has always taken place, and was not an arbitrary process. One consideration is the witness of previous generations to the power which the traditions have to convey meaning and to be engaging, making a claim on one's commitment. This power may not be the *only* consideration but it is significant for without it the recollection of traditions and the roots of one's culture becomes the soulless repetition of the detritus of the past.

This emphasis on the power to convey and give meaning will cause concern on two points. First, in education should one not eschew making claims on the commitments of students and pupils? Secondly, does the emphasis on meaning-giving not lead to an incipient relativism and subjectivism? In answer to the first point, one might ask whether it is possible, or even reasonable, to avoid making claims on the commitments of students. It should be recognised that educational institutions and the educational process are not ideologically neutral. In a pluralistic society therefore it is essential for educational institutions to be ideologically self-critical and to provide as far as is possible an *impartial* analysis of the claims made on human loyalty. Both are necessary if the institutions are to serve the identity and humanity of all.

Whether religious education can legitimately be taught in the secular institutions of a secular state is a question to which Howard Marratt addresses himself. Undoubtedly the character of the state and institution constrains the content and method of religious education. It is in the nature of religion to address itself to human commitment and to pursue a particular form of life. The fundamental religious impulse is not intellectual speculation and theorising. If the religious form of life is briefly defined as 'spirituality' the problems raised by the intentional nature of religion, and thus of religious education, might be eased if spirituality in turn is clearly seen to imply a recognition of mankind's common humanity and a fostering of the unity of all human beings.

In answer to the second point (that to emphasise in religious traditions the power to convey meaning seems to imply subjectivism and relativism), it should be pointed out that this is only possible if the question of truth is either irrelevant or if the truth could never be determined. Mr Hardy attempts to provide a framework in which truth and meaning-giving are seen to be interdependent. If this is possible then the privatisation of religion is to be resisted, and religious education becomes a serious public enterprise.

A popular proverb states that 'if something is worth doing, it is worth doing well', to which has come the retort, 'if something is worth doing, it is worth doing badly'. Presumably the latter exhorts us to life and action and not to take criticism so seriously that one is emasculated and incapacitated from doing anything. This is a timely reminder for those engaged in religious education, but it should not prevent one from seeing that what is done, can be done better. Professor J. Lähnemann provides a contribution with practical guidelines. His sensitivity to the growing Muslim population in West Germany indicates a way in which religious education may be better served, even if it will never be done in a manner beyond criticism.

Education and Diversity of Belief

Paul H. Hirst

Certain diversities in beliefs and practices are commonplace in contemporary pluralist or open societies. But what is the place of such diversities within education? Are they to be tolerated? Indeed, can they be tolerated? Or are they to be welcomed? Are they even necessary to any education worthy of the name? In seeking to clarify these issues I wish to distinguish four different notions of education and the place diversity of belief and practice has within these. But a number of preliminary points will perhaps help to locate the central discussion.

I take it that all notions of education arise because human beings develop as persons by learning and not by mere physical maturation. We become persons at all, and achieve the particular characteristics that distinguish us from each other, because we acquire vast batteries of concepts and beliefs, items of knowledge, patterns of emotional response, attitudes, values, skills, dispositions, habits and so on. Education is thus the process by which each of us becomes the particular person he does, with his own distinctive way of life, an unending process from the cradle to the grave. Further, I shall take it that the cognitive elements that each of us acquires are central to, and determine the character of, all the the other elements of this vast array of achievements. All our emotions, skills, dispositions have the particular features they do in significant part because of the conceptual distinctions and beliefs that are necessary to them. Each of these distinctively human kinds of development is impossible without the cognitive core that it presupposes. And yet further, I shall take it that all these elements are learnable because they have been achieved within the construction of publicly shared languages, patterns of behaviour and institutions. They are all part of what Karl Popper calls the Third World.[1] Not that learning is a simple, passive process so that we become merely the selection of the elements of the Third World that we absorb. Learning that is formative of the person, in the achievement of concepts, understanding, skills and so on, is an absorbing, active business that demands the exercise and progressive structuring of the individual's natural capacities and powers. Only thus can we achieve what the elements of the Third World make available. And each of us too can add his own mite to the further construction of the Third World. But few of us seem able to contribute anything that is significantly new to that World and our originality is, for most of us, to be found in the unique selection of the elements of that world that structures our lives and the way we individually deploy these. Education, then, I shall take to be concerned with becoming a distinctive human person, in the process learning a selection of the elements of the existing Third World.

In addition, it is perhaps necessary to make it explicit that in this paper I shall be primarily concerned with education that is deliberately and intentionally planned whatever the agency. In this sense education is undertaken by parents and priests and the members of voluntary organisations of many kinds as well as by teachers and instructors. Schooling in particular is only one part of education, that conducted in institutions deliberately set up by a society, or groups within it, with particular programmes of learning activities in mind. But it should not be forgotten that within all planned education, and in schooling in particular, the pupils learn much that is not explicitly considered by those responsible. Equally, all planned education takes place in a wider social context in which pupils learn a great deal by their own initiative or in a totally unplanned way. My discussion here will, in the first place, be about planned education in general with wide ranging interests in the cognitive, affective and connative development of individuals. In the second place, I shall comment on certain issues in schooling on our particular form of contemporary society.

The education individuals are offered will clearly vary according to the elements of learning which it aims to bring about. The selection of these elements can be looked at in terms of the general principles involved or examined for specific detail. For the present purpose I wish to distinguish four notions of education based on different principles for selecting the learning aimed at. These are being examined because each rests on a distinctive view of the foundations of knowledge and belief, with resulting differences in attitude to disagreements in belief and their significance in society. In distinguishing these four positions, I am concerned in the first place with the logical distinctions between them, and they are therefore, in the jargon of sociologists, 'ideal types'. In practice, education may be conceived on any or none of these 'models', or on some compromise between them. Of the four, two can be seen as at extreme ends of a continuum, the others being placed at particular stages in between. Throughout I am not concerned with any one religious or non-religious point of view. In particular, amongst the adherents of each major world religion can be found those who will defend each of the four positions.

Education I, or the traditionalist concept of education as I shall sometimes label it, is concerned with the transmission of a body of specific concepts, beliefs, values, skills and so on within a particular tradition.[2] Knowledge and belief from traditional sources are considered justified and valued because of their proven worth across a long period of time. Down the ages they have been tested as instruments of explanation, prediction and control in relation to the natural environment, the individual and society. What is held true or valuable within the tradition provides the content of instruction for successive generations, a content to be accepted by those generations on the authority of the tradition or as resting on certain grounds which that tradition accepts. Within an overarching framework of beliefs and practices some innovation and adaptation to circumstances may be possible; but diversity of beliefs and practices is generally seen as a weakness within the system and likely to lead to social instability. This approach is thus both intellectually and socially conservative in its implications. The idea that the major truths and values for human living have been achieved or revealed once for all forcefully discourages innovation. The appeal to the test of time for beliefs and values makes contemporary difficulties or inadequacies in these seem relatively trivial. Above all, the system contains within itself no challenge by way of deliberately sought alternative beliefs, no self-critical monitoring procedures and no questioning of the over-arching framework. Slow, almost imperceptible, adaptation and reinterpretation by a consensual process are the only likely forms of change. The idea of a pluralist society is not usually part of such a tradition, though specific elements of pluralism may be tolerated. Education in these terms, however, seeks centrally to transmit a total way of life in detail, confining children to the framework of a single and largely monolithic world view. It takes its form from a specific tradition, be that, say, Christian, Jewish, Muslim or Communist, and it is directed to ways of thinking, feeling and acting designed to promote individually and socially the way of life of that tradition. In methods it is likely to favour the procedures of exposition, instruction, catechesis and indoctrination. In a pluralist social context, such education is likely to be ghetto-istic, concerned to preserve the tradition against other possibilities, favouring a large measure of social isolation and possibly indifference, even hostility, towards others.

   Education in these traditional terms has received its strongest support from those who hold that in the last analysis all knowledge and understanding rest on cognitive presuppositions or commitments which man may or may not make, different traditions presenting alternative foundations which are in crucial respects mutually incommensurable. Such an extreme position is, however, hard to sustain convincingly. That men are capable of developing shared concepts and beliefs, that they share the same physical and mental characteristics and are in an environment with largely common properties, means that there are a priori and empirical grounds for maintaining that they must share many elements of understanding. We live in a world. . .

   filled with middle-sized (say between a hundred times as large and a hundred times as small as human beings), enduring, solid objects.

These objects are interrelated, indeed interdefined, in terms of a 'push-pull' conception of causality, in which spatial and temporal contiguity are seen as crucial to the transmission of change. They are related spatially in terms of five dichotomies: 'left'/'right'; 'above'/'below'; 'in-front-of'/'behind'; 'inside'/'outside'; 'contiguous'/'separate'. And temporally in terms of one trichotomy: 'before'/'at the time same time'/'after'. Finally, (we make) two major distinctions amongst its objects: first, that between human beings and other objects; and second among human beings, that between self and others.[3]

All this marks out a domain of what Professor Robin Horton has called 'primary theory',[4] about the physical world, ourselves, others and society that all men would seem to have to share. What is more, elements within such a primary domain are logically prior to and presupposed by all the more complex, abstract and over-arching beliefs and values that are distinctive of the sciences, religious beliefs and other higher level forms of thought. This primary domain is therefore autonomous over against all such abstract systems of theorising. What is true or false in it, what is justified or not, rests on shared common public criteria and evidence. Primary beliefs, knowledge and understanding are thus not peculiar to any particular traditional belief system, but are necessarily common to all such systems once they articulate the relevant areas of experience.

But if such a domain of autonomous understanding, free of any commitment to one specific tradition, is recognised, there is granted too the possibility that areas of abstract theoretical knowledge can develop grounded in 'primary theory' only and not in the other abstractions of traditional systems with which they may or may not be consistent. Indeed, the development of the physical sciences, concerned strictly with abstract understanding in which experiment and observation are the critical tests for truth, bears witness to just such development of understanding that is in logical respects independent of the abstract belief claims of all traditional belief systems. And with such a development emerges very starkly a quite different view of knowledge and belief. What is handed down in a traditional system comes to be seen as limited and possibly quite flawed in important respects. By direct observation and experiment the sciences, in explicit dissociation from traditional beliefs, and generating their own abstract concepts, are able to achieve greater and more accurate understanding of the physical world. There thus arises a progressivist view of knowledge in which innovation and challenge to existing beliefs is positively beneficial.[5] Instead of seeking to maintain consensus of beliefs, competition of rival beliefs put up for public testing becomes recognised as the road to the very goals traditional beliefs have sought – explanation, prediction and control. By challenging each other to explain more and more, rival beliefs provoke the further examination of experience and the extension of experience by using testing processes that are not part of every day life. Launched on this course, it is surely impossible to reject the cognitive superiority over the traditional approaches of this progressive, open-ended, internally competitive and self-critical approach to knowledge with its tests tightly related to the meaning of the concepts in which its beliefs are formulated.

Once grant that neither the basic common understanding of primary theory which is open to all nor knowledge of the physical sciences rests in any way on the abstract beliefs of any traditional system, and education in these areas can no longer be legitimately approached in traditional terms.[6] The concepts, beliefs, values, skills, dispositions involved will all then need to be presented as anchored in a constant concern for immediate experience, alternative beliefs, open critical debate and the revision of beliefs in the light of publicly shared evidence. And just this 'progressivist' or 'critical rational' approach in these areas is one of the marks of what I will label *Education II*, the second of the four notions of education that concern me. On this view there is a common-sense or basic education that can be common to all irrespective of their adherence to a religious or traditional belief system. In the sciences too there can be common educational ground because of their acknowledged autonomy. In these areas, voluntary agreement on the basis of public evidence is what is sought. In these areas, alternative beliefs can be entertained if only because the grounds on which all should agree on the conclusions are openly available to all, at least in principle. And if on some matters the public evidence is inadequate, then in these instances pluralism of belief can be accepted as thoroughly legitimate. But the other mark of Education II is that it recognises this progressivist approach only in the areas of basic common understanding and in the sciences. Outside these the traditional approach holds sway. Literary studies, matters of morals and religion are not considered rational in the same sense as basic understanding and the sciences. In these areas it is only within a particular tradition and commit-ment to its claims that truth and value are to be found. Independent, public-shared criteria not being possible, no resolution of diverse beliefs is attainable in open, competitive debate and education in these areas must therefore reflect that position. Education II is thus split in two. At times it emphasises observation, experiment, discovery, the testing of rival beliefs and theories, critical discussion. At times it stresses exposition, instruc-tion, catechesis, indoctrination and the development of understanding, attitudes, values, experience within the concepts and beliefs of one tradition.

But such a stark split in approaches must surely be unsatisfactory; indeed, it must make education an internally unstable process. If basic common beliefs do not themselves rest on the authority of a tradition, but are rather presupposed in all traditions, and if scientific beliefs that develop out of basic beliefs are equally logically independent of traditional beliefs, what other areas of independent beliefs are possible? Might not complex critical rational understanding of a progressivist nature be devel-oped in matters of moral value, religious belief, social principles or literary judgements? Is it not possible that, when rightly understood, justifiable beliefs in these areas must also be able to survive appropriate forms of open critical public tests? Indeed, is it not the case that such autonomous areas of understanding are in fact being developed? But further, is it the case that beliefs can be isolated into two distinct camps to be approached so differently within education? Are not religious and moral beliefs so closely interlocked with beliefs about the physical world that open-ended challenge to some of the elements of a traditional belief system in scientific terms must infect the rest of the system with critical questioning? And perhaps more fundamentally, once the idea of an individual holding beliefs open-endedly and self-critically is established, is there not something improper, even sub-human, about holding beliefs of any kind in any other way? Is there not something about the nature of beliefs and their significance in human life that makes assent on grounds other than personal critical responsibility improper? In the light of these difficulties, it seems to me Education II offers a crude and inadequate response to the difficulties encountered by traditional education. Some more unified notion must be developed. Those holding firmly to a traditional view of religious, moral and related beliefs have therefore made various moves in attempts to 'accommodate' claims to autonomous beliefs to a traditional system. The resulting forms of education I shall refer to as examples of *Education III*.

At the simplest level, there are attempts to legitimise autonomous beliefs by insisting that the accepted traditional belief system itself recognises the existence of autonomous knowledge. Paramount examples are when the book of Genesis or the Qur'ān is held explicitly to sanction the pursuit of the physical sciences and man's control over the natural world. Such an appeal is often linked with a forceful insistence that traditional values must restrict the pursuit and application of scientific knowledge.

A further unifying move is the claim that the autonomous pursuit of knowledge is only possible within certain systems of traditional beliefs, those which stress the objective existence of the world through a doctrine of creation. Most fundamental is the claim that to pursue autonomous knowledge is but to commit oneself to one 'tradition' which has its own presuppositions. This is then viewed as no more acceptable than any other tradition, each having legitimacy as a point of view, revealing its own distinctive truths and values. If then the 'tradition' of autonomous knowledge is limited in its scope, which indeed it is, it must be seen as subservient to the more wide-ranging power of a richer system.

By insisting on the validity of a traditional approach and on its over-arching higher level importance, Education III can, however, be seen as basically a re-assertion of Education IV in a way which 'domesticates' to its own ends the claims of autonomous knowledge. Such modern traditionalism is in fact no answer to the claims of autonomy, as it mis-understands their nature even in its most fundamental attempts at accommodation. It is simply not the case that the elements of primary theory, and the basic elements that generate empirical knowledge, are presuppositions that may or may not be accepted in a manner parallel to the acceptance or rejection of the fundamental religious and moral beliefs of a traditional system. Rather, these elements can in no way be rejected by any concerned to understand objectively their world and themselves. The claim is that they involve universal forms of conceptualisation that are the product of the exercise of man's natural abilities in interaction with his environment. In that case, rather than elements of such knowledge being rejectable when in conflict with traditional beliefs, they constitute a knowledge base with which traditional beliefs must be consistent if they are to continue to be defensible. Not that traditional belief systems of any sophistication are in sharp conflict with primary theory and the basic elements of the sciences. They have long since been built into these traditional systems. What is unfortunate is the failure of traditional systems to recognise the existence of autonomously-grounded universal elements within their beliefs, and the power and significance of such knowledge once it is explicitly and systematically pursued in its own right.

If the domain of physical sciences has come about by the development into abstract theory of elements in primary theory concerned with the physical world, I see no reason to think that man's abstract theorising in morality, religion, the social sciences has not similarly developed and that within every tradition. What is crucial, however, is whether or not in any context that development has been pursued in a way in which truth can be distinguished from error, the justifiable from the indefensible, by the exercise of appropriate forms of objective and critical judgement. These non-scientific areas certainly involve their own distinctive basic concepts and seek their own criteria for objective judgements related to these concepts, but it seems to me simply a mistake to see these areas as generated in some non-historical fashion or as fundamentally non-rational in character. Of course, some of these forms of conceptual development are concerned with man's own beliefs about himself, and there may be no totally external critique of what is claimed. Equally, they may be seeking to capture elements of experience which are beyond any adequate conceptualisation and thus in an ultimate sense a mystery. But none of this means that there are no rational critical procedures linked to these beliefs. Indeed, their very intelligibility demands that beliefs be consistent and coherent with justifiable beliefs of other kinds. In these very controversial areas beliefs can be more or less rational in certain respects. What is more, I can see no reason why in these areas, as in the sciences, alternative beliefs do not necessarily operate in competition with each other for mutual appraisal in terms of their adequacy in providing understanding and explanation of human behaviour. If they are all extensions of primary theory just as the sciences are, the same demand that they be subject to appropriate open-ended critical assessment must surely apply. That process may well not result in bodies of unique truth. In some areas decisions between alternatives may not be possible even in principle. But that does not mean that anything is acceptable as a valid claim to truth.

If the attempt by traditional belief systems to domesticate the autonomous development of knowledge and understanding fails at this most fundamental level, it surely fails in its more superficial efforts. The values and beliefs of a traditional system may influence contingently the development of the sciences or any other area of autonomous knowledge, but

they are not therefore significant in determining the nature of that knowledge, nor are they relevant to the truth or falsity of any claims in that area.
The truth claims of the sciences stand irrespective of any climate of beliefs
that may promote or hinder their pursuit. Similarly the 'sanctioning' of
autonomous pursuits within a belief system is an irrelevance – autonomy
of its nature denies the significance of any such 'legitimation'. Of course,
in practice the pursuit of knowledge in some area of, say, science or social
enquiry may be rejected on moral or religious grounds. If that rejection is
appropriately justifiable, so be it. But that in no way impinges on the
autonomy of the pursuits in character and achievements, nor does it in any
way vindicate the claims of any particular traditional system as such.

From these comments it will be clear why the approaches of Education
III seem to me to be spurious answers to the challenge autonomous knowledge presents to traditional education. At the same time I have indicated
to some extent the approach to knowledge and belief that I consider must
now characterise any coherent form of education. What is needed is a concept of education that does justice to our contemporary understanding of
the historical construction of all conceptual schemes, their necessary features, and the general characteristics that claims to the justification of
beliefs must have, no matter what form of beliefs we are considering. I
propose therefore that we should henceforth pursue *Education IV* which
is based on the following considerations.

First, all areas of beliefs, values, attitudes and so on are seen as areas in
which rational critical appraisal of what is claimed must be central simply
by virtue of the cognitive claims made, it being understood that the
specific logical form of such rational criticism will vary from area to area.
Secondly, in many areas beliefs and values may not be rationally assessible
as true or false but rather as more or less defensible, and in some cases
several equal rationally-acceptable answers may exist. Thirdly, in certain
areas, notably those of moral and religious beliefs, it must not only be
recognised that particular beliefs are contested, but that there is more
fundamental disagreement concerning what counts as 'rational criticism'.
In these areas, understanding may be reaching the limits of our capacities.
Fourthly, in the development of a society based on justifiable beliefs and
values, it is not possible for any society to begin from scratch.[7] All that is
possible is the piecemeal criticism of the existing system seeking to
modify it progressively into a more defensible structure. A rational society
needs a body of generally agreed principles and practice – for example, a
common language or languages, an agreed economic framework, a body of
common law and a set of agreed political institutions and procedures. It
needs to institutionalise and protect open, critical rational debate
concerned to achieve maximum voluntary agreement. Where agreement
is not attainable it will seek to permit diversity of belief and practice as far
as possible, but will have rational agreed procedures for decision-making
where diversity is not acceptable. How much diversity is acceptable in a
society is itself a disputable matter which must be decided by a rational
procedure. What a society committed to developing a justifiable pattern
of life cannot accept are those activities which will undermine the open

public pursuit of critical reason in all areas.[8]

Within this framework, Education IV will seek that, in all areas, beliefs, values, attitudes and so on are held by individuals according to their rational status, there being a fundamental commitment to the progressive rational development of personal beliefs and practices rather than uncritical adherence to, or determined defence of, any particular set of beliefs and practices whatever their source. As, however, from birth children learn many concepts, beliefs, values, attitudes, habits and so on long before their abilities to assess these rationally are effectively developed, education must operate within a specific context of these elements, yet aim too to develop rational criticism of them. If education must start within some system of beliefs, it is not itself aiming at the maintenance of that system. It aims at the development of the rational life by every individual whatever form that may come to take. Not that any individual can personally achieve a grasp of the justification of everything believed and practised. There must be a rational acceptance of authorities, though that demands that the authorities have the appropriate credentials and that their conclusions are always open to public critical assessment. Education IV is in principle an open-ended pursuit that accepts and seeks to promote diversity of beliefs and practices where reason admits such diversity. But in seeking to be determined by the bounds of reason and reason alone, Education IV must not be thought to be aiming at pupils achieving a general state of critical scepticism or doubt in any area. What it aims at throughout is commitment in belief and practice in every area – commitment by the individual to the most rationally justifiable beliefs and values as he can judge these in his particular circumstances. Commitment and holding to the revisability of that commitment are in no sense incompatible. True, critical assessment of a belief demands entertaining the idea of rejecting that belief, but the 'suspension of belief' for the purpose of critical assessment is not of itself to withdraw commitment, or to enter a state of doubt for any purpose other than that of critical review.

The selection of achievements that education in these terms aims at is not determined by any particular belief system. Education IV is therefore not Christian, Muslim, Marxist, Humanist, or Secularist. In the areas of moral and religious beliefs and practices the aim is, as in all other areas, the pursuit of understanding and personal commitment to what is judged to be most defensible. That commitment recognises the importance of rational critical dispute and the logical status of different beliefs, including those personally accepted. Where personal response goes beyond what critical reflection warrants, just that must be acknowledged. Such a position is not incompatible with commitment to certain formulations of Christian, Muslim, or other beliefs which see these as rationally defensible in some form of open critical debate. Nor is it incompatible with certain notions of revelation. It is compatible with a child being brought up as a 'rational' Christian or Muslim and continuing as such, but it is equally compatible with such a child coming to reject his previously-held faith. Education in these terms is also not incompatible with, though it does not itself include, the activities of, say, Christian evangelism or catechesis, activities undertaken from a committed Christian point of view, provided these are not conducted so as to prevent or undermine a rationally developing commitment.[9] If 'indoctrination' is understood as seeking the holding of beliefs so that they are immune to rational criticism, then Education IV is opposed to all such activities in any context.[10]

Clearly many institutions can contribute to the development of the rational life which can, in the current state of religious debate, take on a number of different religious expressions. The 'rational Christian' can recognise the full legitimacy of a 'rational Muslim' position and other parallel positions. One can therefore envisage as part of Education IV a form of religious education which can be common to members of very diverse faiths and those who reject such faiths, provided they accept a rational critical approach to this area. Religious education of this kind must, however, accept full pluralism and open critical dialogue within a domain where basic critical principles are themselves in dispute. This is not to regard all religions as equally true or false, or to consider commitment as unimportant. It is rather to explore the significance of commitments and non-commitments in the interests of individual judgement, recognising that participants may bring to the enterprise very varied commitments which may or may not undergo change. In such religious education, as in education in all other areas, the critical examination of alternative beliefs and their implications will be an essential part. But even if such an activity is not inconsistent with the retention of a rational commitment to, say, Christian beliefs, the activity itself must be sharply distinguished from Christian catechesis simply because the two operate from different bases. The one does not necessarily presuppose any one particular religious position; the other does and is in fact appropriate only for those who share that as a conclusion. Institutions committed to catechesis from a particular religious position must therefore strongly distinguish those activities from religious education if they support education in the terms here being advocated. To fail to do that is to fail to promote adequately the development of rational faith.

If one turns now from these general considerations to their application in our own social context, it is as well to realise from the start that no complex society is organised in a fully coherent way. Over a long period its institutions and way of life have been modified progressively and they are therefore marked by inconsistencies and pragmatic compromises. Certainly in matters of religious and moral beliefs our response to differences has been not a little confused. In particular, the practice of schools in moral and religious education varies widely. What ought to be done in our maintained schools, if that is democratically determined in free, open, critical debate, must be a compromise which is more or less acceptable to as wide a public as possible, a public in which are to be found all the four concepts of education I have outlined and no doubt many others as well. Progressively in Britain we have moved towards a more open society held together by a common language, common economic practices, common law and political institutions, with at least a significant set of under-pinning common values. Those values are in general directed to achieving consensus in public life by means of critical, rational debate, and accep-tance of differences where agreement in debate is not achieved. This is thus in general a context in which critical rationalism of the kind I have outlined as underpinning Education IV can flourish, it being protected from at least some of its major enemies. In our schools there is now, by and large, a theoretical acceptance that education should be of the open, critical, rational variety that I have outlined, except in the area of religious education and attendant aspects of moral education. In these areas existing legislation at least implies that specifically Christian education should be the norm, though there is a certain tolerance of diversity of belief by means of a conscience clause for withdrawal of children from such religious education and the right to establish voluntary-aided schools on particular religious bases. However, that very tolerance provides no escape from the fact that the schools are not even in principle committed to the demands of open, critical, rational education in these areas. What is more, these particular forms of tolerance are themselves a positive encour-agement to forms of Christian intolerance within religious education in maintained schools, and to the running of religious voluntary schools along the lines of Education I, II and III. Such voluntary-aided schools seem to me not only to offer an indefensible form of religious education, but to be inconsistent with the principles that should govern an open, critical, rational and religiously pluralist society.

But what attitudes to our present maintained school system will adher-ents to my four notions of education adopt? Those concerned with some form of Education I, education in a traditional system of beliefs, must find themselves in serious difficulties with much that goes on in County main-tained schools. They must find the open-ended, critical, rational approach in many areas unwelcome, and the more traditional approach to religious education they are likely to find quite inadequate or contrary to their own particular beliefs. They are therefore going to seek to establish distinctive voluntary-aided schools, or to withdraw from the maintained system altogether. Whatever they do, they are however likely to find that the syllabuses of the public examination system and influences on pupils from our open society outside the school will cause them many problems. Those concerned with Education II will find less difficulty with the education offered in County maintained schools, particularly at the primary stage. But in certain areas, particularly those of religious and moral education, they will encounter the same problems as those holding to a traditional approach. They are therefore once more likely to want some sort of separate schools, but may be prepared to settle for the County school, perhaps using the 'conscience clause' and adding some form of 'supplementary school' provision offering additional part-time education of a traditional kind. Such additional instruction in the evenings or at weekends can seek to complement or act as an antidote to those areas in which County school education is considered inadequate. Those concerned with Education III will vary in their reactions according to the particular form of over-arching traditional beliefs they embrace. For some the separate school will be imperative, for others supplementary provision will be enough.

Those concerned with Education IV will surely seek to modify maintained County schools so that their work in religious and moral education, as in all other areas, is determined by an open, rational, critical approach. Any possible complement to that in terms of the promotion of any particular religious way of life they will wish to keep sharply distinct from the directly educational function of the school, and on a strictly voluntary basis. Where separate schools for particular religious groups are concerned, they will, I suggest, be strongly opposed to these on three major grounds. First, they will tend to be inadequate in their support of open, critical, rational education, particularly in areas of religious and moral education. Secondly, the committed ethos of the school will restrict undesirably the choice of children in important aspects of life when they should be open to a variety of influences within the generally agreed framework of the common morality of the society. Thirdly, such schools necessarily encourage social fragmentation in the society along religious lines. The pluralism of a system of separate schools seems to me to be not the pluralism of a positively-developing rational critical society, for such a society will wish its major institutions to encourage unity amongst its members, a unity born of an open, rational, critical approach to all of life's concerns.

But an existing open society may not at any one time support a thorough-going version of Education IV. If so, the more's the pity, for to my mind Education IV is the only coherent stance that does justice to the very nature of human knowledge and belief. In the end, just as within education science has to be recognised as a progressive, self-critical, rational pursuit, so must religion, morals and all other genuine pursuits of understanding. And only then shall we be on the road to a proper recognition of the place of diversity within education. For that place must be determined by the role of diversity of belief in the open pursuit of truth, and by an awareness of the limits there are to man's capacities to reach truth and therefore properly to restrict his own and others' way of life.

Notes and References

1 POPPER, K. R. (1972) *Objective Knowledge*. Oxford: Oxford University Press (chapters 3 and 4).
2 In this section I am further developing a distinction I have previously drawn, notably in *Moral Education in a Secular Society* (1974; London: Hodder and Stoughton), chapter 5, between a primitive or traditional approach to education and a sophisticated approach concerned with developing rational autonomy. In this I have drawn heavily on the paper by ROBIN HORTON, 'Tradition and modernity revisited', in HOLLIS, M. and LUKES, S. (eds) (1982) *Rationality and Relativism*. Oxford: Blackwell. Outlining my own position, however, has involved

abbreviating and adapting elements of his illuminating analysis in ways he might well not accept.

3 HORTON, R., ibid., page 228.

4 HORTON, R., ibid., page 228. On the status and character of primary theory, see also the comments by Dr Steven Lukes in the same volume: 'Relativism in its place', in HOLLIS, M. and LUKES, S. (eds), op. cit., pages 272-3. On this matter I side with Dr Lukes.

5 For the major contrasts between what Professor Horton calls 'traditionalistic' and 'progressivist' concepts of knowledge, see pages 238-58 of his paper (op. cit.).

6 On the cognitive superiority of the 'progressivistic' concept of knowledge, see HORTON, R., op. cit., especially page 248. As will be seen later in this paper I do not share his conclusions on the achievements of the 'progressivist' concept in the domain of social life. See also Dr Steven Lukes's comments on this issue (LUKES, S., op. cit., pages 298-305).

7 See POPPER, K. R. (1957) *The Open Society and its Enemies*. London: Routledge and Kegan Paul (especially vol. 1, chapter 9).

8 For an excellent outline and defence of the features of a pluralist society committed to critical rationalism and of the demands that makes on education, see CRITTENDEN, B. (1982) *Cultural Pluralism and Common Curriculum*. Melbourne: Melbourne University Press.

9 For a further discussion, see HIRST, P. H. (1981) 'Education, catachesis and the church school', in *British Journal of Religious Education*, Spring.

10 See SNOOK, I. A. (1972) *Indoctrination and Education*. London: Routledge and Kegan Paul.

A Response to Paul H. Hirst

Kevin Nichols

I am by trade a country parson. I don't apologise for that; but country parsons are supposed to stick to writing hymns, studying natural history and composing stylish diaries. They aren't supposed to mix it with the rather abstruse and certainly logically complex questions which Professor Hirst has raised in such a clear and challenging way. The general theme which holds these thoughts together, is an attempt to relate the conflict or complementarity between catechesis and education with the conflict or complementarity between faith and reason.

When we go back into the early history of the Christian Church, we find that many of the Fathers who shaped its thought would have agreed with Professor Hirst's sharp distinction between catechesis and education, though they would not have thought of the two as complementary. On the contrary, there was a strong school of thought (including St Jerome) which wanted converts and catechumens to have nothing whatever to do with the Greek Schools. The liberal learning they offered would only cloud the saving wisdom of the Cross. However, other counsels, represented by Origen and Clement of Alexandria, prevailed. Well-catechised Christians could benefit from Greek scholarship. They would know how to make the necessary discriminations. They could even despoil the Egyptians. It was a case of Education II fading into Education I. When the Christian Church came to control education, type I became established. Theology was to be the capstone of the house of intellect; Education was to serve catechesis. We find this synthesis in Aquinas, we find it also in Newman. Yet Newman was not an Education I person. Although Theology was queen, the autonomy of other disciplines was to be respected. It is no part of the business of Theology to go trampling over other people's gardens.

In his lectures on 'the scope and nature of University Education', Newman shows an unusual ambiguity, indeed a change of direction. In the first half, the 'philosophic habit' is a noble thing, almost like faith. In the second half, no, perhaps it is not. Perhaps its practitioners are 'victims of their own intense self-contemplation'. Perhaps what is needed is a 'vastly more superstitious, more bigoted, more gloomy religion'. One critical turning point in the history of the Christian Church was its adoption by Constantine which put it squarely in the market-place of social institutions. Another was its massive investment of faith in the bank of Aristotle. Between them, these two moves brought about the powerful but basically unsteady predominance of the Christian Church in Western education. Philosophy was long regarded as the handmaid of Theology. Yet the time of its emancipation was bound to come when the slave would compel the former mistress to learn her letters. Education equally was bound to discover its own independent life and become secular. Newman's hesitations about the synthesis were symptomatic within the Christian community of a widespread pastoral and theological unease with it. Still, despite retreats into fideism, into traditionalism, or into pietism, the long wrestling between faith and reason, between catechesis and education, continues.

Next, I should like to take up something Professor Hirst said about tradition. The Christian idea of tradition, if I've got it right, is not the handing on of a static and completed package like a baton in a relay. It is more like a living and organic growth; an 'idea' as Newman said, which in its history, goes through many changes of expression. Consequently, induction into a tradition can allow leeway for growth and change and makes room for personal autonomy. Is it, however, as Professor Hirst asked, reviseable in principle? If 'in principle' means root and branch, then evidently not. For tradition is a compound of continuity and change. But if 'in principle' means that each expression of the tradition is open to criticism and reformulation in ways which do not contradict the central expressions of the past, then tradition is so reviseable, provided the criteria of continuity are fulfilled: preservation of type, continuity of principle, power of assimilation, logical sequence and so on. Hence catechesis induction into a religious tradition is not necessarily at the bottom of Division IV, constantly having to apply for re-election; it isn't a pure case of Education I. Its goal has been described as 'free adherence to God in faith',[1] an idea which should respect and promote autonomy rather than suppress it. So if it is wholly separate from education, this must be because its material content is not accessible to public tests and cannot find any secure foothold among the forms of knowledge.

Now I have two observations about the position of religion among the forms of knowledge. First, I should like to draw on Newman's thoughts again. Against the evidential theory of Locke, Newman argues, 'he consults his own idea of how the mind should act, instead of interrogating human nature as an existing thing'.[2] Men do make religious assents, both real and notional. They have evidence which should be taken seriously. But it should not be confused with empirical evidence and it does depend in some way on moral dispositions and the reasons of the heart. Notional assents may rest on a secure ground of evidence. They are abstract and lead to repose, which is why, Newman says, intellectuals are rarely devout. Real assents are the main concern. They involve struggle, commitment, action, even a 'perilous substratum of doubt'. Should the religious teacher concern himself with these?. Or where beliefs differ widely, should he restrict himself to the notional? Is it religion as dull habit? Or is it religion as acute fever?

John Hick, admiring Newman's method and approach, thinks he is mistaken in taking propositional religion as the main and typical kind.[3] It is a case of type fallacy. It is true, I think, that Newman overvalued doctrine, or mistook its place among the dimensions of religion. Yet in spite of that he had a view of cognition which involved feeling, moral sense and action, which looked ahead to the work of Kierkegaard and Blondel. Religious truth is best found in autobiographies and novels. 'It is the whole man that moves. Paper logic is but the record of it. You might as well say that the mercury in the barometer changes the weather.'[4] Truth embodied rather than truth discussed will be the main concern.

This view of religious knowledge moves it a good deal closer to the aesthetic form than to any other. In literary criticism, public tests and evidence do exist, however difficult it is to formulate an unvarying method. My old teacher F.R. Leavis used to say that every critical judgement ended with an unspoken 'This is so, is it not?: an invitation to assess evidence and raise further questions. However hard pressed, he would not be pushed to formulate the 'ideas' or 'position' of a writer in a philosophical way. The words on the page are the data. The intelligent, sensitive communicated and discussed response is the method. It was a classic instance of the literary form of knowledge.

Many theologians at present, especially those interested in religious education, give great prominence to the idea of 'story'. A network of narrative, character, event, action and feeling forms the personal story of each of us. This personal story is 'named' in relation to the 'great story' which is its archetype. In this process of 'naming', the critical question arises in which intelligence and sensitivity are alike deployed; this is so, is it not? This approach to religious education might be characterised in the phrase 'the ministry of the imagination'. Here I take imagination in Coleridge's sense: a creative power which fuses diverse elements into new meaningful totalities.

However, this approach to the religious form of knowledge applies only to one of the dimensions of religion – the mythic one. Is religion then to be parcelled out, each of its aspects being subject to difficult criteria, truth-tests, evidential rules? Up to a point, the phenomenon of religion is bound to be analysed from several very different points of view. But this would not result in fragmentation if, instead of a relatively relative structure of the forms of knowledge, there existed a unified theory of human cognition which showed invariant features. Bernard Lonergan has attempted to work out such a theory.[5] For him a single pattern can be discerned in the very various ways in which the forms of knowledge go about their business, a pattern which is summed up in the precepts: be attentive, be intelligent, be rational, be responsible. For Lonergan, faith will not be complementary to reason. It will be another instance embodying the fourfold structure of human understanding. The difficulty many will find in this idea of faith as a form of human cognition is its connection with conversion of heart and commitment. However, in Lonergan's view of human understanding, conversion is by no means restricted to the religious sphere. He stands at the opposite end of the epistemological spectrum from those who hold that knowledge is a social construct. It is not that he would deny that knowledge is often organised and ranked by the power of social structure. But these cases, he would say, are examples of group and general bias, examples of the difficulty men experience in keeping intelligence central to human life. 'The hopeless tangle of the social surd, of the impotence of common sense, of the endlessly, multiplied philosophies, is not merely a cul-de-sac for human progress, it is also the reign of sin, a despotism of darkness; and men are its slaves'.[6] These powerful words are not recommending an evangelical purgation. They assert rather that there is a movement of conversion in all true cognitional activity: intellectually from general and individual bias towards attentiveness, reason and judgement; morally from egoism towards rational responsibility; religiously from partial insights to the primary, intelligible, invulnerably known through the knowledge which arises from love. Thus conversion, far from being anti-educational, becomes a necessary educational goal at every level. It is, moreover, a single process though embodied in several forms, and through it the chasm between overt religion and that which is implicit in human experience is bridged.

Finally, and very briefly, may I indicate some practical consequences which might arise from this line of thought.

First, religious education could deal in real assents: that is, personal commitment could be deployed as a resource, provided, of course, that the vulnerability of children is respected and, of course, that the teacher is prepared to risk himself as well.

Secondly, there could be a dialogue in education between different traditions within the mental world of faith, parallel to the theological dialogue with the religions of the East conducted by Raymond Panikkar, Bede Griffiths and others. The approach of 'sharing and passing the story'[7] would support this.

Thirdly, it is a line of thought which opens the way for an 'experiential' as well as a 'phenomenological' approach: that is, taking the raw material of religious education to be the ordinary data of experience rather than overtly religious phenomena. A unified theory of understanding would be one which supports a grasp of the same data from progressively higher viewpoints. And, finally, an education based on that theory might, precisely by virtue of being invariant in its features, provide the best approach to religious education in a pluralistic society.

References

1 SACRED CONGREGATION FOR THE CLERGY (1973) *The General Catechetical Directory* (paragraphs 20, 86). London: Catholic Truth Society.

2 NEWMAN, J. H. (1870; 1889) *The Grammar of Assent*. London: Longmans Green (chapter 6, page 164).

3 HICK, J. (1966) *Faith and Knowledge*, 2nd edition. Ithaca, NY: Cornell University Press (chapter 4).

4 NEWMAN, J. H. (1864; 1955) *Apologia Pro Vita Sua*. London: Dent (page 163).

5 LONERGAN, B. S. F. (1958) *Insight, a Study of Human Understanding*. London: Darton, Longman and Todd.

6 LONERGAN, B. S. F., op. cit., page 692.

7 PANIKKAR, R. (1964) *The Unknown Christ of Hinduism*. London: Darton, Longman and Todd.
   GRIFFITHS, B. (1976) *Return to the Centre*. London: Collins.

Can Theology have an Educational Role?

Karl-Ernst Nipkow

I have been asked to draw on my experience, in the World Council of Churches and in Germany, to illustrate how, on the one hand, in public education institutions attempts have been made 'to develop the religious nature (spirituality) of students, and on the other hand, how theological thinking has attempted to meet educational concerns'. I shall focus on the role of theology in a classroom with students who are of another religious tradition or from a secular background. How, if at all, can and does theology perform an educational role in such a pluralistic situation?

1 Religious Education in the Public School System of the Federal Republic of Germany

Since the sixteenth century (the Reformation) the transmission of Christian faith to the younger generation has been institutionalised in Germany in two main forms: *Church Education* (*Firmungs* – and *Konfirmandenunterricht*) in the local congregations for about two years (ages 13–14 for Protestant children) and *Religious Education* (*Religionsunterricht*) in the public (state) school system for all years (ages 6–18). Religious education is confessionally bound: Roman Catholic and Protestant. It must be offered to the students, thus being *obligatory* for the school as an institution. But it can be refused by the parents or by the students themselves (from the age of 14 onwards), therefore it is *voluntary* from the side of the pupils.

Since the time of the Weimar Republic (1919–33) these regulations express a political compromise between two demands. On the one hand, there is the public interest in leaving religious education as an integral part of the school (as before), in accordance with the two main historically-rooted confessions, and on the other hand, the individual right of religious liberty in a country which now has a separation between State and Church. For this reason, the article on religious education in the Federal Republic's constitution (Article 7 *Grundgesetz*) is placed in the essential introductory part which deals with fundamental human rights, the Basic Rights (*Grundrechte*).

The legal understanding of the idea of freedom of religion underlying these rules is the notion of 'positive religious liberty' (positive *Religionsfreiheit*). The state, though abstaining from identifying itself with any particular religion, positively provides opportunities for young people to come into contact with and to practise religion. Consequently, any religious organisation can demand to be represented in schools provided that it meets certain basic corporative conditions as to number of members, stability and so on. With approximately 1.9 million Muslims living in West Germany, the debate is now about the possibility of religious education for Muslim students in the state school system, in addition to the private Qur'ānic schools which already exist.

2 The Pluralistic Religious Scene – Erosion, Differentiation and Transformation

In the West German context as outlined above the challenge to the role of Christian theology is not only the presence in the classroom of students from another religious background who come from other living faiths, but also, over a period of many years, a growing presence of students from a secularised Christian background with a polymorphic secularised religious pluralism. Now can this pluralistic scene be described?

Its dominant signature is not shaped by militant non-Christian or non-religious ideologies like the militant atheism, liberalism, or Marxism which attacked the churches in earlier periods of German history (for example, the '*Kulturkampf*' at the end of the nineteenth century, or during the Weimar Republic). The churches today are not opposed by visible enemies with a profiled ideological identity.

What we find in our society, and what is mirrored by the students in our schools *and* in our confirmation classes, is a growing process of erosion of traditional piety, doctrinal orthodoxy, and loyal church affiliation. However, this process does not result in pure agnosticism, but in a great diversity of more or less subjectively worked out forms of religiosity and its functional equivalents. The whole cannot be explained only by autonomous individual decision-making, rather, structural social factors must be taken into account.

(a) Among these determining factors underlying individual behaviour social disintegration must be noted. No single social institution on its own is able, or even attempts, monopolistically to provide answers to everything. The attempt to find an integrated view of life as a whole is left much more than in former times to the individual: it becomes a matter of private freedom of choice. (On the theory of social differentiation and its consequences for religion, see Luckman, 1967; Berger, 1979; F. X. Kaufmann, 1979; and most recently Drehsen, 1983, page 175).

(b) A second structural factor is the loss of organisationally exerted social power ('Disorganisation', Drehsen, 1983, p. 177). Our liberal German church organisations have been affected by this general opening of our world and contribute to it by their very nature as '*Volkskirchen*'. People belong to them by birth (by baptism as a social Christian convention), and as adults, regardless of what their factual religious behaviour may be, or what their principles of life may look like (faithful to the church or not), they will not be socially controlled, either by the public or by the church (with one exception, namely the obligation to pay church-taxes). Theoretically, this loss of social control leads to the same private freedom mentioned in (a) above. As a matter of fact, the individual does not become totally independent, because numerous competing general world-interpretations, reflected in their eclectic use by others, are around him/her, half-consciously or openly inviting him/her to form a view of his/her own. These influences include the traditional and modernised belief-systems of the churches; other secular and religious life-interpretations (humanistic or socialistic ideologies, and, of growing influence, 'new religions' and psycho-religious 'human potential' movements); above all, the popularised views of the natural and social sciences.

Viewed sociologically, this loose organisational framework of our churches favours and even necessitates, as its counterpart, not only individualised forms of religiosity, but also 'group-religiosity'. Whilst large organisations function with a very low need of articulated consent and active engagement, religious groups need both.

Within our West German '*Volkskirchen*' we meet a large variety of more or less group-bound types of Christian piety and spirituality, in particular on the left and right wings: fundamentalistic Bible-oriented and evangelistic-missionary groups, liturgical movements emphasising the eucharist, prayer, meditation, some charismatic renewal groups, women's spirituality, theologically motivated 'third world' initiatives, and, last but not least, Christians in the peace movement and in new ecological life style experiments including monastic communities.

It is important to see that much of this is highly attractive to young people. In the upper levels, the teacher of religious education will meet, at least to some degree, a spectrum reaching from the 'church-faithful traditional' youth (more in rural areas), across the broad middle field of 'church-critical worldly' Christian youth (mostly in urban areas), to the new and old groups of left and right wing attitudes, if this grouping may be allowed.

(c) The deepest and presumably most decisive reason why theology is confronted with this secularised differentiation is the result of cognitive dissonance. This third factor means that if people compare the traditional doctrines of the churches with the thought-patterns of scientific world interpretation, they feel as if they should live in two different worlds, or 'two different ontologies' (Schmidtchen, 1973). There is a similar discrepancy in the field of value-system (Forster, 1973; Schmidtchen, 1972,

1973, 1979; Hild, 1974; Feige, 1982). Several values of high priority for young people (and adults) will not be the value priorities of the churches ('to be a free and independent person'; 'to enjoy life, to be happy').

To overcome both the cognitive dissonance and the discrepancy of values, people will usually establish a new balance for their identity by giving up that position which is supported least by their near social reference-groups (family, relatives, friends, colleagues). For youth, friends are the strongest negative factor potentially urging them to drop their church loyalty (Feige, 1982, page 37). Many students in religious education, so we may conclude, share the attitudes of the broad mass of church-alien and church-critical nominal Christians, who are more or less affected by a process of the growing obsolescence of church doctrine and values, except for love (Feige, 1982, page 305). The popularised objectives by modern critiques of religion and critiques of ideology add to this break-up of the Christian tradition. The result of all this, however, is not so much a life in a no man's land, as a heterogeneity of diverging ways of thinking though still within the loose frame of the '*Volkskirchen*'. Principally, the Christian faith is one option beside other non-Christian options, just as traditional Christian ecclesiasticism is only one option beside other secularised Christian options. The signature of our religious scenery can be considered as a decline of religion only if seen from the angle of a traditional theological self-understanding and measured by the frequency of church-attendance. More adequately, the situation can be described as a transformation of religion in a time when the substance of Christianity, particularly in liberal Protestantism, is set free to enter new amalgamations with pieces of other traditions and styles of thinking, floating around for private usage.

3 From 'Training' to 'Problematising' Transmission of Christian Faith – the Fundamental Change of Paradigm in Post-War Religious Education in West Germany

Given these conditions, how are theology and religious education to react? In the Federal Republic, where religious education is anchored in Christian confessions and is obliged by constitutional law to be given 'in accordance with the principles of the religious societies' (Article 7, 3 *Grundgesetz*), everything depends on how these principles will be interpreted theologically.

In our century, the answers given by Protestant theology to which I shall mostly, though not exclusively, refer are very illuminating. In the first two decades of our century the answer was a theological affirmation of 'modern' educational demands. Protestantism was seen more or less in consonance with the age ('*Kulturprotestantismus*'), in accord with the scientific spirit of modern times as well as with the liberal ideas of the beginning of a new era, including reform in education (compare J. Dewey,

E. Key, M. Montessori *et al.*). Protestant theologians propagated a 'modern sermon' (Niebergall, 1905) and a 'modern religious education' (Baumgarten, 1903).

The decades after the end of World War I were marked by an interruption of this process of modernisation. The understandable reaction of so-called *Dialectical Theology* against any theological adaptationism and the consolidation of the church during the 'Church Struggle' (*Kirchenkampf*) after 1933, rallying faithful Christians with the experience and vision of the church as a true community of believers in Christ, ready to resist all powers of dissolution, led to a corresponding 'closed' type of Christian education and instruction which after World War II was deliberately given a new name, no longer 'Religious Education' (*Religionsunterricht*) but 'Evangelical Instruction' (*Evangelische Unterweisung*) (Kittel, 1947).

This period was to last until the end of the fifties. Church and school religious education was based on the identity of theology and the life of faith. The classroom should become a part of the living church ('church in the school'). The teaching-learning paradigm was a sort of 'training transmission' by which some might have hoped and may still hope to stop the decline of traditional ecclesiasticism and religious differentiation (see above, page 24). The characteristics of this 'training' and 'integrating' type of transmission were: the integration of the students into the life of worship within the classroom by praying and singing, a proclaiming, missionary style of Biblical instruction, and a positive transmission of doctrine. As regards the children and youth, they were expected to be ready listeners to the Gospel (Rang, 1939), while the teacher was called upon to act as a witness.

Following the fifties, a fundamental change in religious education in schools has gradually taken place. Usually this period is considered only as a time of reform, whereas I venture to claim that what has emerged during the last 25 years is in fact a change of the paradigm. The overall societal process of problematising Christian church-bound belief-systems became the topic and even the function of religious education itself. The new type of faith-transmission is now no longer a sort of 'training' and 'integrating', but, paradoxically, a 'problematising' transmission. The religion to be transmitted is deliberately and explicitly displayed as problematic. Before describing this shift in detail, I will offer one preliminary theoretical remark. The last two and a half decades show the emphatic interest in developing a theory of religious education which has a dual base. Research has drawn upon the two disciplines of Theology and Education. The postulate of a dual legitimation does not mean a simple doubling of arguments. If this were the case, theology might soon become redundant and replaceable. Rather, a two-fold question must always be posed. On the one hand, can theology, by its own strictly theological reasons, demand that educational criteria be valid for religious education? And, vice versa, can education, by its own strictly educational reasons, support the claim that theological criteria be observed in religious education (Nipkow, 1969)? Such a theoretical approach, known as the *convergence model* (for elaboration, see Nipkow, 1975, I, page 173, II-III), does not look for the lowest common denominator; rather, the two questions simultaneously make visible the abiding differences between education and theology. In linking both *correspondences* and *differences*, it has been denominated a pattern of 'dialectical convergence' (Nipkow, 1975, I, page 177).

(a) To begin with the *legitimation of the existence of religious education* in the secular school system: why religious education at all? The breakthrough was made by Martin Stallmann in his book *Christentum und Schule* (1958). As the title indicates, the school is addressed as school with educational arguments. The school is confronted by the theologian with the postulate that true education cannot do without the interpretation of human history and tradition which reflects the permanent endeavours of human beings in their emphatic and often desperate search for the truth of life. The Christian tradition can serve the school in this purpose not as the only, but as an exemplary, field from which to learn, a paradigmatic field of radical questions and answers.

The new point in this argument is that the school is not urged to permit religious education because the churches want to teach the Gospel to baptise students. This line of argument is completely dropped. Rather, the school is educationally urged not to neglect the deeper level of interpreting life and existential self-understanding by reducing instruction to a shallow acquisition of functional knowledge. Most illuminatively, this educational argument is paralleled by a theological one (dual legitimation, see page 27 above) from two directions. In the light of Friederich Gogarten's later theological views, the history of secularised Christianity is seen not just as a deplorable process of growing 'secularism', but also as the legitimate history of the consequences of the proclamation of the Gospel in the 'secular world' (apart from Stallmann, 1958, see also Otto, 1961, page 45). This new theological appreciation of 'secularisation' (as opposed to 'secularism') means that the subject-matter with which teachers in religious education have to deal is not the 'Word of God' itself (which for Stallmann is adequately transferred only in the sermon as personally addressed *viva vox evangelii*: Stallmann, 1963), but it is 'religion', in this case 'Christian religion', treated like any other historical religion. Therefore the old name 'religious education' (*Religionsunterricht*) is correct (Stallmann, 1958).

Karl Barth's fight against 'religion' by separating 'religion' and 'faith' is still deemed justified in the *soteriological* dimension in so far as 'religion' is understood as a human instrument of self-redemption. But this notion of 'religion' must be confuted. Barth's separation is wrong in the *hermeneutical-didactical* dimension, and this is the primary dimension in religious education by the very nature of instruction itself. Here the 'Word of God' as the word of salvation is at our educational disposal only in the form of 'religious objectivisations' which can and have to be dealt with in the same instructional manner as other subjects (as, in a way, Barth himself does in *Kirchliche Dogmatik*, I, 1. 1932, page 51).

An additional theological re-interpretation is that the process of searching for meaning in human life uncovers the situation of the person under the 'law' (Stallmann, 1963, page 250).

(b) Secondly, during these same years confessional Protestant religious education in schools was changed in its process structure. Particularly for the upper levels, but also for earlier years of schooling, religious educators demanded that the spirit and method of scientific theological research become the spirit of religious education (Stock, 1959, 1968, and the series *Handbucherei für den Religionsunterricht*, 1965 ff., with publications by Wegenast, Becker, Dignath, Wibbing *et al.*). The methods of 'historical criticism' and 'de-mythologisation' (Bultmann, Käsemann, Bornkamm, Marxsen) were introduced first. Some years later the methods of the social sciences (psychology, sociology, and so on) were added, eventually including even the instruments of Marxist and Freudian 'critiques of religion' (Otto *et al.*, 1972; Vierzig, 1975).

With these developments there was a convergent form of theological and educational reasoning. This combined the reflection on schooling which was increasingly subject to scientific and critical criteria (Wilhelm, 1967; Nipkow, 1968b) with modern biblical exegesis which was self-critical and scientific in character, and with approaches in systematic theology which were both self-critical and openly competing with other scientific interpretations (Pannenberg, 1973).

(c) Thirdly, as to the content of religious education, the sixties brought new topics. The earlier dominant role of the Bible was supplemented and partly replaced by life themes. Much energy was devoted to developing a 'thematic problem-oriented' second didactic type of religious education (Nipkow, 1968a; cf. Kaufmann, Dessecker, Martin, and Meyer zu Uptrup; Berg and Doedens; Biehl, and many others). In relation to the 'texts' of the Bible, this 'context-type' (Nipkow, 1970) has made its way into the new curricula (Larsson, 1980).

New topics do not necessarily imply a new teaching-learning-paradigm. But in this case, the new approach did. 'Problem-orientation' means both religious education on life themes as new curricula items *and* a new way of dealing with these new curricula, as well as with the old curriculum material (the Bible, church history). It is the way already mentioned, the way of problematising transmission (H. B. Kaufmann, 1973). Faith tradition and present reality of life are now confronted in an open-ended process. Secular and non-religious views of life are not introduced as a black foil in order to put the Christian answers in a bright light. The adoption of this strategy, well-known from research on persuasion (Hovland, Janis, Kelley, McGuire), is explicitly refused (Nipkow, 1970, page 276). The Christian interpretation shall be treated as 'one beside others'.

While the convergent argument concerning the present reality draws educationally on modern didactics (Klafki, 1963), it is theologically supported, on the one hand by the new forms of society-oriented political theology in both Protestant and Catholic camps (Moltmann, 1964; Metz, 1968), and, on the other hand by the hermeneutical postulate that an understandable speaking of God must go together with a radical and complete analysis of human reality as the place where the human being's situation will be laid open, and where God wants to be understood (Ebeling, 1960, page 366).

(d) The opening of religious education outlined above leads, fourthly, to a new inner form in the relationships between denominations, religions, and ideologies, the form being a *dialogue*. Here it will suffice to say that it was the Council of the Evangelical Church in Germany (EKD) themselves who officially confirmed that there should be a fair dialogue, not only with other Christian denominations, but also with 'non-Christian religions and non-religious convictions' (EKD-Kirchenkanzlei, 1972).

(e) With regard to the students and the role of the teacher during these years, the expectation of addressing the pupils as little Christians ready to listen to the Word of God and to the doctrine of the church authoritatively taught by a teacher as a witness was abandoned. Questions, doubts, critical remarks of students were now welcomed without any sanction and, more than that, fostered to provide for an atmosphere of freedom and credibility. The teacher in religious education was now seen as an 'interpreter under the conditions of non-belief' (Stock, 1959, page 157), the student as a 'modern human being' (ibid.).

(f) Finally, on the level of aims and objectives, a spectrum of realistic aims replaced the former theological and ecclesiastical homogeneity, which had gone far beyond the possible. Surprisingly enough, it was the Joint Synod of the Catholic Dioceses in West Germany (Gemeinsame Synode der Bistümer, 1974) which affirmed that religious education should take account of *all* types of students; those faithful to the church might be helped to become more rooted in their Christian faith 'by a more reflective decision of their own', those full of doubts might be given the opportunity 'to learn about the answers of the church to their questions', and as for non-believers, religious education might assist them 'to see their position more clearly' (page 18). Thus the Roman Catholic Church moved in the same direction as the Protestant.

4 The Two Types of Theology – 'Positional Identity' and 'Critical Dissociation'

I shall conclude in two stages, one of explanation and one of discussion.

How can the new role of theology in modern West German religious education be explained? We obtain some illumination from the historical nature of theology itself. It is a process of inner differentiation, similar to the process of differentiation in religious life (see above). How could it be otherwise? Theology participates in this process, and the first and fundamental step is the dissociation of religion and theology as such, of the life *of* religion and reflection *on* religion. This dissociation is related to the emergence of science itself.

Hans Urs von Balthasar (1960, I, page 224) observes the transition in medieval times from a 'kneeling theology' to a 'sitting theology'. The first, the monastic type, is largely an act of praying faith, the second, scholastic type is an attempt at systematically objectivising knowledge about faith. The theologian takes a step aside, as it were, now standing beside him or herself, giving up the former identity, at least to a certain degree. Today, theology as an academic discipline participates in this separation by systematically reflecting and critically checking the forms of 'faith-theology-identity', and hereby more or less dissolving this identity – a permanent source of possible temptation for the pious believer and of possible irritation to the official church authorities. In church history, however, again and again pietist movements have tried to bridge the dissociation of religious life and theological reflection, of faith and theology, in order to 'return Christian thought and Christian life to its original unity' (Rössler, 1978, page 510; Drehsen, 1983). It stands to reason that the church as an organisation has an interest of its own in securing this integration, for doctrinal reasons.

Thus we face two general types of theology. The first is the more or less immediate cognitive articulation of living piety. Theology becomes a way of proclaiming faith – religious education likewise, if such a model is followed, will take the form of proclamation. This sort of theology, resting on the inner identity of theology and faith, must necessarily split up into as many different theological positions as we find different faith positions, be it the dogmatic positions of a denomination (church-bound 'confessional theology'), of a movement ('pietist theology', 'charismatic theology', 'political theology', 'theology of liberation', 'black theology' and so on), or of individual Christians as theologians (cf. Rössler, 1970).

The other type differs from the first not by lack of the positional engagement of faith as a personal attitude of the respective theologian, but by the way this engagement is critically reflected upon by means of rational criteria and controlled in the medium of scientific theological research, open discussion and metatheoretical methodologies. This second type is diversified, too, partly because of the continuing side-effects of the personal faith position and church affiliation of the theologian, partly because of differences in scientific methods, approaches, and results.

Both types, the one characterised by 'positional identity', the other by 'critical dissociation', can and do have an educational role, as I have illustrated. Between 1930 and 1960 the first model was dominant in Germany. Later the second model took precedence (see above).

5 The Educational Relevance of both kinds of Theology

Finally, if we discuss both types of theology in relation to the tension between the secular school on the one hand and the development of religious spirituality on the other, we might be prompted to divide up and locate the first type of 'positional, identifying theology' in Church education and Christian nurture, and the second type of 'critical, dissociating theology' in religious education in schools.

This double-track division can be supported by the following arguments. In a state school system of a multi-religious society, if there is only *one* form of *obligatory* religious education for students of different religions, a 'practising' confessionalist teaching-learning pattern cannot be accepted, for educational reasons. Even in West Germany, where legally it would have been allowed, this pattern has not been followed for the past two decades, owing to the principal insights into the nature of today's conditions under which people as individuals make – and have to make – a choice of their own. The sociologically demonstrated degree of differentiation and subsequent pluralism, and the cognitively proved degree of controversy in matters of religious belief, necessitate an open, informing and self-critical 'problematising' type of faith transmission. This option can be additionally supported by the theological consideration that the Christian understanding of faith implies a free and personal belief (Nipkow, 1975, II, page 99).

However, it has to be admitted that this approach of critical and enlightened religiosity is, from another perspective, restrictive in its educational effects. Students will be stimulated to think about religion, but will not be very emotionally touched by religion. If one compares the classroom constraints with the possibilities of church youth work, for instance, community experiences in the different forms of camping and adventure trips, of festivals and liturgy, of learning by living together and by doing project-work, one might say, at least in the case of West Germany, that these latter forms probably have a greater integrating power, while religious education in schools has a more clarifying function. Therefore there is some truth in the double-track strategy just mentioned, but only some truth.

First, there is the same general social context of religious differentiation and cognitive dissonance (see above). Both the young people in confirmation classes or in church youth programmes and the young people in the religious education classes share the same spectrum of attitudes.

Secondly, there are similar risks; the risks one might run with an open religious education (students turning their backs on church and religion because of a certain relativism and cognitive doubts) will be balanced by the risks in a closed church education (turning one's back on church and religion because of possible intellectual submission and monopolistic narrowness). As far as we can see in the Federal Republic, the results of religious education are encouraging (Feige, 1982); the results of a more conservative church education are not (Hild, 1974; Feige, 1982).

Thirdly, in both places, in church and religious education, children and youth expect and need the strengths of the two approaches: the openness and reflection of the self-critical type of theology and the living authenticity and positionality of the other type, and of their corresponding forms of teaching and learning. It is necessary, for educational reasons not only for theological ones, to stress the strengths of both types of theology, by offering to students free space which allows them to compare several positions, and by helpful orientation, presenting one position with which to identify. 'Integrating' and 'problematising' experiences in the field of religion do not exclude each other. On the contrary, they form a necessary productive polarity which, if institutionally and legally possible, should be taken up everywhere within one and the same institutional context – that is, in church education and in religious education in state schools. High educational value has to be given both to the spirit and methods of self-critical Christian theology and the substantial traditions of positional Christian theologies.

Why and how do both ways of theological work and of corresponding Christian education point to each other? Why do we have to think complementarily? What we have differentiated analytically belongs together in substance in several respects which need to be elaborated.

From a developmental point of view, children do not start their lives with critical openness and rationality. The small child in particular, but the older child no less so, needs the basic experience of living in a reliable, safe and unambiguous world which is not permanently questioned (Langeveld, 1956). The courage to let go of mother's hand, or to be out of sight of father's watchful eye is rooted in the experience of a given security – the child knows that he or she can run back home at any moment. Processes of emancipation in physical and mental respects, discoveries in space and mind, remain bound to the awareness of belonging to someone and to something. This is also true of the religious life. Just as we would readily grant to non-Christian pupils in a multi-faith society the need to become and remain rooted in their own specific religious heritage, so we ought to acknowledge it also for Christian children.

As regards young people, it seems to be wrong to assume that the main developmental task is only the search for identity in the form of individual independence. There is to the same degree the deep and, in later adolescence, growing expectation of finding people to whom one can belong and with whom to share a communal conception of life. This is also valid for the religious sphere. It is the 'new religious movements' in particular which show the constitutive importance of 'groups' and 'group-religiosity' outside and within the churches (for a general sociological analysis of the role of 'family-like' intermediate social structures, see Coleman, 1982).

Recent research on the moral development of female youth (Gilligan, 1982) illustrates that girls in particular look not only for identity as autonomy, but also for the experience of intimacy and of responsibility of being cared for and of taking care of others. 'Intimacy precedes, or rather goes along with, identity as the female comes to know herself as she is known, through the relationships with others' (Gilligan, 1979; page 437). Thus experiences like love, tenderness, care, compassion, responsibility play a great role as well. If we apply this to the field of religion, we see that those features of religion may become important which embody and release 'non-rational' values, values of 'the *ratio* of the heart'. These are not to be found in any theology of rational and objectifying study (the 'sitting theology' of 'critical dissociation'), but only where theology is identical or at least comes near to committed religious life itself (the 'kneeling theology' of 'positional identity').

And the adults? What do we know about the growth of faith? For a mature stage of faith, neither a one-sided commitment by merely 'dwelling in' a specific religion nor the attitude of objectifying and demythologising aloofness are characteristic, but a 'conjunctive faith' as a synthesis of a specific religious commitment with, and at the same time, a deep understanding of, and even personal affection towards, other religions (Fowler, 1981).

It is not only our children and youth who need the strengths of both types of theology and their corresponding forms of religious education, but also society and its state school system. Once more it has to be said first, that the general school system of a nation in the Western world cannot allow any values to be the leading ideas other than the spirit of freedom and tolerance, of reconciliation and humanity. Here also religious education has to follow, as have all other subjects. The school cannot become a battlefield in a fight to win souls. Instead, all religions which want to be represented in the school curriculum must be asked if they can join a pattern of teaching and learning that obeys the rules of objectifying analysis and open discourse. The answer will depend on the self-understanding of each religion.

In modern times, step by step most of the Christian churches have taken up in their theological work the spirit and the criteria of the modern academic search for truth; justifying it with theological reasons, they can give a positive answer without being forced to contradict themselves and to give up their basic convictions. In religious education in state schools (and in Christian nurture as well!) the churches not only can but must support a liberal approach because a message that speaks of the person's liberation by God and of God's will for reconciliation is not allowed to be transmitted by unfree methods. In this paper we assert that Christian theology can meet the basic educational needs in an open society while nevertheless still remaining Christian theology (see above). Whoever would deny this from a philosophical point of view would be wrong, and one must assume that his/her image of Christian theology is merely following an understanding of it as something dogmatic in an irrational and narrow-minded sense. My differentiations above are intended to correct this possible view.

But what about the 'positional' forms of Christian theology, or a corresponding 'positionality' in other religions (Judaism, Islam, Hinduism and others)? The state school system is entitled to reject any 'confessionalist' dogmatism, but it should invite the religions to say what they have to say substantially, provided the overall spirit of freedom and tolerance in the school will not be violated (see above). The reason is that we all, young and old, need to know what is born from the deepest grounds of each religion as its own voice, and what these voices have to say to the burning issues of our individual *and* collective life – therefore their legitimate place is not only in the private sphere but also in a public institution like the school. Many people in our societies suffer from a crisis of meaning of life. Meaning (*Sinn*), however, cannot be produced either administratively or by the formal arrangements of an open, universal discourse alone; critical rationality is a necessary but not a sufficient condition. Moreover, our societies are far from embodying true social justice, in particular in their relationship to the so-called Third World. They are basically divided and shattered by the issue of nuclear armament and the search for peace. They are faced with the forces of self-destruction in ecological problems and so on.

Here and elsewhere, religious experience can add to the dialogue needed. 'Dialogue' as the signature of an open society presupposes identifiable dialogue-partners. Dialogue implies *positionality*; the way of discovering the common good (to introduce the younger generation to this process is one of the pre-eminent tasks of a state school system) does not lead into a region beyond controversies and separations, but is dialectically to be found in spite of and through them.

If we finally see together the developmental and the societal reasons outlined above with their implications for religious education, the school should offer and initiate both, positional religious and moral interest (and even commitment) within an atmosphere of religious openness and mutual understanding. As to the organisation of religious education, it would be adequate to combine forms of specific religious education (Christian, Jewish, Muslim and so on) mainly for the younger pupils, with joint sessions creating the opportunity for multi-faith experiences and encounters mainly for the older. Everyone knows how exciting it is to participate in, or listen to, panel discussions between members of different religious affiliation where positionality *and* self-critical, objectifying analysis become a reality. The same is true on a more emotional level through mutual invitations to religious feasts. But whether one can follow this pattern of a 'mixed' organisation or not – and its implementation depends on the given constitutional, legal conditions – the general line of the argument should have become clear: the necessary and possible educational role of theology exists in more than only one way, namely, in self-critical openness and in spiritual commitment. Both are essential as the expression of a worldwide ecumenical learning process in a world of different denominations, religions, ideologies and cultures.

The complementary links between the two sides which we have discussed, between positional religious identity and mutual religious openness and understanding is reflected in the following observation of a young Turkish citizen (aged 20) in my country: 'Between Muslims and Christians there are of course differences. But if one thinks about them, it becomes more important to discover how people may live together. Being firmly rooted in one's own faith helps one to deal with one another in a more human way. I know a lot of people who as Christians go to church once or twice a year, but who are rather ignorant about their religion. With these people it is difficult to come to a true understanding of their religion or humanity' (Newzat Teker).

References

BALTHASAR, H. U. von (1960) *Verbum caro. Theologische Skizzen I.* Einsiedeln: Johannesverlag.

BARTH, K. (1932) *Kirchliche Dogmatik.* Trans. Bromiley, G. W. and Torrance, J. F. (1956–62) *Church Dogmatics.* Edinburgh: Clarke.

BAUMGARTEN, O. (1903) *Neue Bahnen. Der Unterricht in der christlichen Religion im Geist der modernen Theologie.* Tübingen/Leipzig: Mohr.

BERGER, P. L. (1979) *The Heretical Imperative.* Garden City, NY: Doubleday.

COLEMAN, J. S. (1982) *The Asymmetric Society* (The Frank W. Abrams Lectures). Syracuse, NY: Syracuse University Press.

DREHSEN, V. (1983) 'Protestant piety movements in the process of modern social differentiation.' *Social Compass,* XXIX, 2–3, 167–87.

EBELING, G. (1960) *Wort und Glaube.* Tübingen: Mohr. Trans. (1963) *Word and Faith.* London: SCM Press.

EKD-KIRCHENKANZLEI (ed.) (1972) *Die evangelische Kirche und die Bildungsplanung.* Gütersloh: Mohn; Heidelberg: Quelle and Meyer.

FEIGE, A. (1982) *Erfahrungen mit Kirche. Daten and Analysen einer empirischen Untersuchung über Beziehungen und Einstellungen junger Erwachsener zur Kirche.* Hannover: Lutherisches Verlagshaus.

FORSTER, K. (ed.) (1973) *Befragte Katholiken – Zur Zukunft von Glaube und Kirche.* Freiburg/Basel/Wien: Herder.

FOWLER, J. W. (1981) *Stages of Faith. The Psychology of Human Development and the Quest for Meaning.* San Francisco, CA: Harper and Row.

GEMEINSAME SYNODE DER BISTÜMER IN DER BRD (1974) *Der Religionsunterrichte in der Schule.* Heftreihe Synodenbeschlusse Nr. 4. Bonn: Sekretariat der Synode.

GILLIGAN, C. (1979) 'Woman's place in man's life cycle.' *Harvard Educational Review,* 49, 431–46.

GILLIGAN, C. (1982) *In a Different Voice. Psychological Theory and Women's Development.* Cambridge, MA: Harvard University Press.

HILD, H. (1974) *Wie stabil ist die Kirche? Bestand und Erneuerung. Ergebnisse einer Umfrage.* Gelnhausen/Berlin: Burckhardthaus.

KAUFMANN, F. X. (1979) *Kirche begreifen.* Freiburg: Herder.

KAUFMANN, H. B. (1973) *Streit um den problemorientierten Unterricht in Schule und Gemeinde.* Frankfurt: Diesterweg.

KITTEL, H. (1947) *Vom Religionsunterricht zur Evangelischen Unterweisung.* Berlin/Hannover/Darmstadt: Schroedel.

KLAFKI, W. (1963) *Studien zur Bildungstheorie und Didaktik.* Weinheim: Beltz.

LANGEVELD, M. J. (1956) *Kind en religie.* Utrecht: Erven J. Bijleveld.

LARSSON, R. (1980) *Religion zwischen Kirche und Schule. Die Lehrpläne für den evangelischen Religionsunterricht in der Bundesrepublik Deutschland seit 1945.* Lund: Gleerup; Gottingen/Zurich: Vandenhoeck und Ruprecht.

LUCKMAN, TH. (1967) *The Invisible Religion.* New York: Macmillan.

METZ, J. B. (1968) *Zur Theologie der Welt*. Mainz: Grünwald; München: Kaiser. Trans. (1973) *Theology of the World*. London: Burns and Oates; New York: Seabury Press.

MOLTMANN, J. (1964) *Theologie der Hoffnung*. München: Kaiser. Trans. (1967) *Theology of Hope*. London: SCM Press.

NIEBERGALL, F. (1905) 'Die moderne Predigt.' *Zeitschrift fuer Theologie und Kirche*, 15, 203–71.

NIPKOW, K. E. (1968a) 'Christlicher Glaubensunterricht in der Sakularität – Die zwei didaktischen Grundtypen des evangelischen Religionsunterrichts.' *Der Evangelische Erzieher*, 20, 169–89. [NIPKOW, K. E. (1971) *Schule and Religionsunterricht im Wandel*. Heidelberg: Quelle and Meyer; Dusseldorf: Patmos (236–63).]

NIPKOW, K. E. (1968b) 'Der aufklärerische Charakter moderner Pädagogik.' *Die Deutsche Schule*, 60, 149–62. [NIPKOW, K. E. (1971) *Schule und Religionsunterricht im Wandel* (11–27).]

NIPKOW, K. E. (1969) 'Religionspädagogik und Religionsunterricht in der Gegenwart.' *Katechetische Blätter*, 94, 23–43; [(1969) *Theologia Practica*, IV, 215–35; NIPKOW, K. E. (1971) *Schule und Religionsunterricht im Wandel* (161–87).]

NIPKOW, K. E. (1970) 'Beyond the Bible in religious education.' *Concilium*, 3, 6, 43–55. [Enlarged version, 'Problemorientierter Religionsunterricht nach dem "Kontexttypus"', in NIPKOW, K. E. (1971) *Schule und Religionsunterricht im Wandel* (264–79).]

NIPKOW, K. E. (1975–82) *Grundfragen der Religionspädagogik*, vols. I–III. Gütersloh: Mohn.

OTTO, G. (1961) *Schule, Religionsunterricht, Kirche*. Göttingen: Vandenhoeck und Ruprecht.

OTTO, G. *et al.* (1972) *Handbuch des Religionsunterrichts*. Hamburg: Furche.

PANNENBERG, W. (1973) *Wissenschaftstheorie und Theologie*. Frankfurt: Suhrkamp.

RANG, M. (1939) *Handbuch für den biblischen Unterricht*, 2 vols., 3rd edn. 1948. Tübingen:

RÖSSLER, D. (1970) 'Positionelle und kritische Theologie.' *Zeitschrift fuer Theologie und Kirche*, 67, 215–30.

RÖSSLER, D. (1978) 'Frömmigkeit als Thema der Ethik', in HERZ, A. *et al.* (eds) *Handbuch der christlichen Ethik*, vol. 2. Freiburg/Basel/Wien: Herder (506–17).

SCHMIDTCHEN, G. (1972) *Zwischen Kirche und Gesellschaft*. Freiburg/Basel/Wien: Herder.

SCHMIDTCHEN, G. (1973) *Gottesdienst in einer rationalen Welt*. Stuttgart: Calwer.

SCHMIDTCHEN, G. (1979) *Was den Deutschen heilig ist. Religiose und politische Strömungen in der Bundersrepublik Deutschland*. Muchen.

STALLMANN, M. (1958) *Christentum und Schule*. Stuttgart: Schwab.

STALLMANN, M. (1963) *Die biblische Geschichte im Unterricht*. Göttingen: Vandenhoeck und Ruprecht.

STOCK, H. (1959) *Studien zur Auslegung der synoptischen Evangelien im Unterricht*. Gütersloh: Mohn.

STOCK, H. (1968) *Religionsunterricht in der kritischen Schule.* Göttingen: Vandenhoeck und Ruprecht.

VIERZIG, S. (1975) *Ideologiekritik und Religionsunterricht.* Zürich/ Einsiedeln/Köln: Benziger.

WILHELM, TH. (1967) *Theorie der Schule.* Stuttgart: Metzlersche Verlag büchhandling.

A Response to Karl-Ernst Nipkow

John M. Hull

Introduction

Professor Nipkow's paper deals with the relations between religion and education in West Germany. I have been invited to reply to him. I would find it rather difficult to comment at all on the situation of which he has such expert knowledge. I will, therefore, try to do for Britain what he has done so ably for Germany, and my comments will form a 'reply' only in so far as I shall not attempt to construct a carefully argued set of my own ideas but will follow the outline of Professor Nipkow's paper making references to it wherever possible.

1 Some Meanings of the Question, 'Has Theology an Educational Role?'

Professor Nipkow states in his opening paragraph that he has been asked to show how attempts have been made to develop religious awareness in students in public educational institutions. The focus of the question, he continues, will be on the position of theology in the classroom with students who are of another religious or secular background. Thus it would appear that 'theology' refers to the content of what is being taught and the impact of this upon pupils. Although 'theology' does appear on the time-tables of some Roman Catholic secondary schools in Britain, it is normal to describe the classroom activity, the school subject, as religious education.

Professor Nipkow also states that he has been asked to present some ideas about how theological thinking has tried to meet educational concerns. In Britain, 'theological thinking' would be that thinking which is characteristic of theology as a discipline, that is, the thinking which is involved in the articulation of systematic religious belief together with the thinking required by such disciplines as contribute to this or draw inferences from its results. In asking how theological thinking has tried to meet educational concerns one would thus be asking about the extent to which theology has sought to correspond with educational ideas, or make successful relationships with educational concerns. These would include the concerns of religious education, as being part of education. The quest would thus be for a theological rationale for a theory of general education, or the more specific task of providing a theological contribution towards a theory of religious education.

We see, therefore, that the question could either be concerned with the extent to which religious education (if 'theology' equals 'religious education') can be justified by educational norms (that is, whether religious education has a truly educational task), or with the extent to which, or the way in which, theology (theological studies, theological thinking, the systematic articulation of religious belief) can contribute to the formulation of a theory of education in general and/or religious education in particular.

It is also possible that the question as to whether theology has an educational task could be an invitation to consider whether people can learn from theology itself. Theology may present itself as being 'saving belief', but we might ask whether, in addition to its soteriological role, theology also has an educational role. Does theology as practised in the church and in universities, and as the self-conscious reflective life of a faith, have any place as a model of how education should take place? Can theology become a learning resource for modern people?

These, then, are the three main ways in which our question could be understood, and it is worth emphasising that these three meanings are quite separable in the sense that each question could be pursued without any reference being made to the other meanings. In the next section we will consider the second of these meanings: the possibility that theology could provide a rationale for education and hence for religious education.

2 Theological Thinking about Religious Education

As has been said, in the United Kingdom the classroom subject taught in primary and secondary schools is only occasionally called 'theology'. In general, religious education would not be regarded as being theology, or as being an example of theological thinking. Theology might, of course, be part of what was presented in religious education classes – for example, the theology of the Fourth Gospel, or 'trends in modern Christian theology'. It is also the case that, whether religious education contains explicit theology or not, it would still be possible to consider the whole of the curriculum, including religious education, as an example of a result of theological thinking, or, at least, as being available in some way for theological evaluation. Religious education, in particular, might be thought of as an application of theological thinking, since on the face of it there are many more points of obvious relation between theology and religious education than between theology and other taught subjects. One could, for example, ask whether the presentation of a certain topic in Christian Studies was theologically satisfactory, and this might mean asking whether the presentation of the topic was faithful to the self-understanding of Christianity, or one might also ask whether the presentation of the topic was adequate according to the norms and values of a particular theological approach within Christianity. One could ask such theological questions not only about the content of religious education but also about its methods, its aims and objectives, the philosophical foundation upon which the work was proceeding, and so on.

It is important to emphasise, however, that in the United Kingdom religious education as a subject taught in the publicly maintained schools is thought of today as being part of the ordinary (i.e. secular) curriculum. To that extent the 1944 Education Act, with its distinction between 'secular instruction' and 'religious education', no longer corresponds to professional practice. This means that a theory of religious education is to be obtained by bringing together those subjects which have a bearing upon the study of education: for example, the philosophy of education, the psychology of education, and so on. This group of contributory disciplines would be no different in the case of religious education from that of any other subject of the curriculum, or from that required by study of the theory behind the curriculum as a whole. So one has a psychology of religious education just as one has a psychology of mathematical education, and there may be philosophical problems in history education just as there will be such problems in religious education. In the same way, theology of education takes its place beside philosophy of education and other such disciplines and, when applied to individual subjects, theology may well have a comment to make upon geography just as it may have comments to make upon religious education. We may speak of a theology of geography education just as we speak of a theology of religious education.

The implications of this situation are not only that theology will be related to religious education in the same way (although perhaps not so obviously) as theology is related to geography, but also that theology is but one of the disciplines which contribute towards a theory of education, whether as a whole, or with respect to these several parts of the curriculum. Although problems in the theology of religious education have a right to be considered separately and to be tackled in the light of theological resources and theological methods, this treatment can never take place in isolation from the other contributing disciplines. Theology of religious education will not only be in dialogue with religious education; it will also be in dialogue with philosophy, sociology, psychology, history and so on. This point is underlined by Karl-Ernst Nipkow when he refers to the concern of contemporary religious education in Germany to base itself in both the theological and educational camps, that is, to draw its theoretical justification and its guiding principles from theology as well as from the education disciplines; or perhaps we should speak of the *other* educational disciplines, since theology may be an educational discipline (see sense three, page 40). I myself believe that we should not separate theology from the educational disciplines but should regard it as being one of them, at least when theology is taking its place alongside educational disciplines and is co-operating in an attempt to create or clarify a rationale for religious education. It may also be the case that when it is being considered in relation to science, theology may then be thought of as being a scientific discipline and we could then ask whether theology has a scientific task.

If there is a slight difference of emphasis between Karl-Ernst Nipkow and myself at this point, it may perhaps reflect no more than the institutional conditions of our work. He is involved in a joint appointment to both a faculty of theology and a faculty of education, and could easily regard his role as relating theology to the educational disciplines. He could thus come to regard theology and the educational disciplines as having some kind of parallel structure. I am working *within* a faculty of education, in a situation where in actual practice theology of education is but one of a number of disciplines contributing towards courses in educational studies. Theology cannot but take its chance along with the others as to its educational relevance and scholarly status.

But I do not wish to lay any emphasis at all upon this little difference, because when Karl-Ernst Nipkow goes on to say that the crucial question is whether theology, by strongly theological reasons of its own, can demand that educational criteria be valid for religious education and, vice versa, whether education, by educational reasons of its own, can support theological criteria, these are just the questions which concern us in Britain as well.

Karl-Ernst Nipkow describes the relationship between theology and education or religious education as one of 'dialectical convergence'. I agree with the description of the relationship, and perhaps it is worth remarking that although I do believe that theology must take its place alongside the other educational disciplines I do not think that the model of dialectical convergence could apply to many or any of the others. Although there is a trend in the psychology of education which takes the classroom situation as the centre of attention, and courses which used to be called 'psychology of education' are often now called 'classroom skills', it remains the case that concepts like 'learning', 'motivation', 'behaviour' and 'concrete operational thinking' are as much part of psychology itself as are any other concepts in psychology. These expressions, whether used of classroom teaching or not, are part of the psychological construct system. But they are also part of the language of Education. In the same way, terms such as 'knowledge', 'mental', 'reason' and 'autonomy' are as much part of philosophy as anything else in philosophy, and they are also terms intrinsic to educational studies. So it is not a matter of taking psychological and philosophical concepts and relating them to educational concepts, for they are already educational concepts. It is not a case of a convergence from what might be thought of as two separable bases. But are there concepts central to theology, or which might be regarded as much a part of theology as anything else in theology, and which are also a natural part of the contemporary world of educational studies? One can, of course, trace all sorts of mutual influences. That is what convergence is all about. But the fact remains that words like 'holy spirit', 'grace', 'sin' and 'salvation' are theological constructs and are not a natural part of the vocabulary of education, whereas words like 'learning', 'development' and 'skill' are (amongst other things) part of the world of education and not central to religious discourse. The truth of this can be seen in any of the works which have tried to systematise the nature of the study of theology in the last couple of hundred years, from Friedrich Schleiermacher to Gerhardt Ebeling.

This 'convergence', distinctive of theology of education, is created by the fact that in theology there is an inside and an outside and this in turn is a reflection of the nature of the church itself and of religious faith. One can choose whether or not to be inside religious faith; one cannot choose whether or not to be inside rationality. Religious faith, in other words, is an option in an altogether different sense from any in which psychology or philosophy might be options. It is in conceiving religious faith as an option that we make it possible for such faith to retain some of its essential characteristics, and for the secular to remain the secular. It is out of this peculiarity of religious faith that the convergent nature of theology in relation to non-theological disciplines springs. It is by realising the nature of religious faith as an option that we are enabled to avoid the claim that all education is necessarily theological, which would lead to the *identity* of theology and education rather than their convergence.

These reflections about method in the theology of general education apply also to the relationship between theology and religious education. Far from being the whole of religous education, whether in content or as providing a theory, theology seeks to establish a critical convergence, not an identity. Theology, which springs from the self-understanding of religous faith, remains an option, in the sense that religious education, like any other secular discipline or enterprise, may get on perfectly well without it. There is nothing about religious education which is intrinsically mysterious, and which might need theology to explain some supernatural variable in the learning process, nor is there anything about the theory of religious education which requires divinity. There is no God of the religious education gaps. The two fields may converge because they do have something in common, but the degrees of convergence will always remain negotiable, and one of the reasons for this is that the common ground is also a homeland for sociology, philosophy, psychology and the other disciplines which seek to illuminate educational practice and theory. Religious education could be taught in a faculty of theology, but it would be difficult for it to avoid becoming didactics or catechetics. It might come to be thought of mainly as dealing with problems of communicating the faith. In the wider context of educational studies and of the entire secular curriculum, religious education is no longer merely an appendage, and theology, while unable to rule, does at least have the advantage of getting in amongst secular thinking and in that way of being where the action is. It is better to be a dog harnessed with other dogs helping to pull a real cart, even if you are a rather peculiar dog, than to be a solitary, performing dog having nothing serious to do in the outside world. It is true that the cart could get along without you (there are other dogs) but in this theory-laden, complex and pluralist world there will always be competition as well as co-operation between dogs.[1]

3 Theology and Religious Education in Britain

Following the outline set by Professor Nipkow, it would be appropriate now for me to attempt some brief description of the relationships between theology and religious education in Britain, by which I mean the way in which trends in theology have influenced the work of religious education in schools. It is probably true to say that this relationship has not been as thoroughly developed in Britain as it has been in Germany. Perhaps the very fact that in Germany religious education has been confessional in the literal sense of that term (that is, it has been directly related to particular confessions of faith such as Protestant or Catholic) has not only permitted but has encouraged a deeper penetration of theology into religious education. In the United Kingdom, however, religious education in the publicly maintained schools has never been specifically related to one particular denomination. The Cowper-Temple clause in the 1870 Education Act forbade the use in the Board Schools of formularies or catechisms distinctive of a denomination, and although the individual teacher was not prevented from expressing his own denominational views, this was defended in the name of freedom of speech and Christian conscience and was not seen as encouraging denominational sponsorship of religious education classes.[2] The much richer doctrinal teaching which accompanied the rise of the agreed syllabuses from the 1920s was certainly influenced by theological trends, but the very machinery of agreement meant that a certain distance continued to prevail between the churches as being the centres of theological reflection and the schools. Only in the independent schools was it possible to work out what a Quaker, or a Methodist, or an Anglican approach to schools and to education might be. There was, in the period between the two World Wars, a vigorous attempt to introduce into the state-related schools (the Local Education Authority (LEA) schools) a model of Christian education based upon the independent schools and this was not entirely without success in creating assumptions about the schools as a Christian community and so forth.[3] Of course, it is true that as the twentieth century wore on, the denominations were no longer the focus of theological renewal, which tended rather to be expressed in movements (such as Neo-Orthodoxy) which cut across them. Nevertheless, the facts that after 1944 the clergy were no longer given the right of access into the schools, that the inspection of religious education passed from the churches to the state, and that a religious education teaching profession began to mature which was based not on ecclesiastical or even theological loyalties but on professional training, meant that theology, whether of the ecclesiastical or the university type, became increasingly diffident about appearing to be too paternalistic towards religious education.

As for the religious teachers themselves, they were trained either in universities where theological departments took almost no cognisance of the fact that these undergraduates would some day be religious education teachers, or in teachers' colleges, where the theological and religious studies were based upon those of the universities. If theology had an application to the professional work of these religious education teachers, it lay in preparing them to teach the content of their syllabuses, and, as far as I am able to discover, there was virtually no attempt to enable religious education teachers to think theologically about their professional work, and to work out the implications of this or that theological emphasis for this or that *kind* of religious education. This is not to say that teacher training in religious education did not carry with it certain assumptions about the religious nature of education as a whole and of religious education in particular, but 'assumptions' is exactly what they were. Theological reflection about the religious education process was almost always instructional, homiletical, or kerygmatic, and hardly ever critical, exploratory, or comparative.[4] Teachers, for the most part, were thus left in a situation or dogmatic naivety or innocent superficiality, and the task of a serious theological contemplation of professional responsibilities was hardly begun. Where such work did take place, it was devotional rather than professional; it sprang from the nature of the teacher as Christian rather than from the nature of the Christian as teacher.

These comments about the limitations of theological reflection about religious education as being due to the lack of an active and institutionalised relationship between the denominations and schools apply more to England than to Wales, Scotland, or Northern Ireland. In Northern Ireland, the fact that Roman Catholics were almost entirely withdrawn from the LEA schools meant that the latter became virtually a Protestant system, which was reinforced by ecclesiastical inspection of these schools. This, combined with other factors peculiar to Northern Ireland, meant that religious education there has always been much more consciously Protestant in the LEA schools, and perhaps one may consider this to be an example of theological influence. Similar situations arose in Scotland and in Wales, not because of ecclesiastical divisions but because of the relative unanimity of the various denominations regarding their religious educational policies. It was in England alone that pluralism, secularism and professionalism combined to create the rather superficial relationships between theology and the classroom which we have been discussing.[5]

In spite of the problems described above, there have been outstanding examples of English theologians who have included education and religious education within their religious thinking. Samuel Taylor Coleridge comes to mind, and so do Frederick Denison Maurice, and

William Temple.[6] We could also consider the impact upon religious education of various understandings of the relationship between Church and State,[7] or different views as to the nature of Christian childhood as expressed in different theories of Christian nurture.[8] We could study the impact upon religious education of Idealism as in the Neo-Hegelian movement in British philosophy and theology during the last quarter of the nineteenth century and on until the 1940s.[9] It would also be possible to show that there was some awareness in British religious education during the 1920s and 1930s of American religious liberalism,[10] and, following this, the influence of Karl Barth and the 'biblical theology' movement into the 1950s.[11] The collapse of many of the old assumptions during the 1960s gave rise to a new interest in theological questions, not least in religious education, and the so-called 'new religious education' of that decade was often linked with the 'new theology' of Bultmann, Tillich and Bonhoeffer.[12] As the options open to religious education became clearer and more diverse towards the later 1960s,[13] there was a deeper awareness of the theological implications of the various approaches, and also a growing desire to establish theological foundations for at least some of them.

The situation in the 1970s was complicated by the emergence of what could be regarded as virtually a new subject, a religious education no longer to be considered as being intimately related to the Christian faith and which increasingly saw itself, at least in some of its emphases, as being beyond theological appraisal. Religious education saw itself as falling under the secular discipline of curriculum studies, and as being generated by the philosophy, sociology and psychology of education.[14] Even the religious subject matter of religious education teaching was removed from obvious theological scrutiny, since that content was now based upon secular and scientific methods for the study of religions – for example, phenomenology.[15] At a time when it was vital for religious education to establish itself as being a genuine part of the educational enterprise and as being sustained by an educational theory which would win acceptance from educators and from teachers of other subjects, theology was seen as a doubtful ally, or even as an embarrassing reminder of a tutelage from which the present subject was not rapidly freeing itself. The entire theology of Christian nurture, which had been the mainstay of the theological rationale for religious education, was now rejected, and in many religious education circles in Britain it was not a question of what theology would fill the vacuum, because the demands of professional education seemed to deny that there could be such a thing as a theological vacuum. It was felt that a theological rationale for the subject would lead to a theological domination of the subject, or perhaps we might say that in many cases there was so little understanding of the role of theology *vis-à-vis* religious education that it was feared that any attempt to include theology among the subjects which would provide for a theory of religious education would lead to a weakening of the claim that religious education (so important if its struggle to survive in the state educational system was to be successful) could be justified on educational grounds.[16] Just as at the time of the Protestant Reformation there were some who cried 'Faith and works' while the more militant cried 'Faith alone', so there were now some who cried 'Theology and education' while the more militant cried 'Education alone'. It was thus often assumed that any appeals to theological grounds or educational grounds for the justification of religious education would be appeals to two quite different types of ground.

We may see this as an attempt on the part of religious education to assert its relative autonomy within the educational realm in the face of the theology which had previously domesticated it. We may, perhaps, also interpret this failure to accept theology as having an educational task as springing from a failure on the part of some religious educators to distinguish between what Karl-Ernst Nipkow has called 'kneeling' theology and 'sitting' theology, that is, a failure to appreciate that theology can take its place alongside the other disciplines, and need not always be in a position of exclusive, adoring contemplation of itself and its objects of faith.

We could also describe these difficulties as springing from a problem in the re-conceptualisation of the role of theology *vis-à-vis* religious education in a period when that role was changing from a consideration of an essentially domestic activity within the Christian church to consideration of a secular activity outside the Christian church.[17] The change required a new understanding of the nature of practical or applied theology, and in a tradition where practical and applied theology had been thought of almost entirely in domestic terms (catechetics, homiletics, pastoralia and ethics) it proved difficult to conceive of ways in which theology could enter again into a fruitful relationship with religious education, now that the latter was no longer to be considered as an aspect of catechetics or of Christian nurture but insisted on being recognised as part of the secular educational enterprise. We must emphasise once more that the fact that the leading approach to the subject since the early 1970s has been the phenomenological approach to the study of world religions has inhibited theologising about religious education. The very emphasis upon a value-free approach to religious studies, and the contrast with theology which was seen as a value-laden enterprise, have encouraged the idea that theology could not contribute to an objective account of religious education; so phenomenology was associated with a professional approach to religious education, and theology was associated with a confessional approach.[18]

Turning next to the contemporary scene, we see many different attempts being made to relate theology to religious education. There is certainly a quickening of interest in this aspect of the foundations of religious education. Religious education scholars with an interest in theology are seeking to establish links between their subject and hermeneutical theology,[19] the theology of liberation,[20] narrative and story theology[21] and so on. We must also consider the interest which Islamic religious educators have in placing not only the study of Islam but the whole of education under theological control,[22] and the work being done on the theological assumptions of a variety of classroom materials, such as theme teaching[23] and the use of parables[24] in the classroom.

A number of factors may be contributing to this new freedom in theological thinking about religious education. Reading Paulo Freire has alerted many religious educators to the social, political and religious values hidden behind an apparently neutral and professional education. The increasing number of religious education specialists who are highly qualified in theology, but who are not ordained, means that the significance of the theological vocation of the layman or laywoman in education is being recognised more and more. No doubt also the recent developments in religious education, which to many theological observers has been unusual if not provocative, have been a stimulus to theological reflection.[25] Not least among these trends has been the emergence of the phenomenological method in the British classroom. Although one suspects that this has been an issue which has attracted the attention of some theologians because of the familiarity of the controversies within theological departments between 'religious studies' and 'theology', and this has occasionally led to an exageration of the significance of this division in religious education, nevertheless it must be listed as a significant factor in helping theologians to realise that interesting theological developments were taking place in the schools.[26] Reference has already been made to the interest of Islamic scholars in education, and it is probably true that religious education in schools has emerged as one of the most interesting examples of the encounter taking place between world religions. This has naturally stimulated an interest in the views of the various religions towards education.[27] No doubt the present freedom and plurality of approaches within Christian theology itself have also contributed something to the sense of openness and variety which is encouraging theological thinking about education.

Having said all this, the interest in theologising about religious education must not be exaggerated. The truth is that religious education studies, like other studies in education, have become more specialised in recent decades. Thus there is not only more interest in what might be called theology of religious education, but there is also more interest in the philosophy of religious education, its psychology and so on. Indeed, religious education scholars tend increasingly to see one of these aspects as being their own major specialism within religious education studies. The interest in theology is thus part of a general maturation of reflection and scholarship within religious education as a whole.

I remarked that these new developments are coming mainly from religious educators with an interest in theology rather than from theologians with an interest in religious education. There are a number of notable exceptions to this, theologians whose main interest is in one of the aspects of theological studies and yet who have made and are making significant contributions to theological thinking about religious education. Nevertheless, in the main, I think that it would be true to say that the gulf which has opened up in recent decades between professional theologians, whether ecclesiastical or university, and religious education has still not been bridged. The nature of this rift between theology and religious education has never received the study which it deserves, but if one reads the fore-runner of the *British Journal of Religious Education* (*Religion in Education*) during the 1930s, 1940s and 1950s, one finds that in issue after issue the most distinguished biblical scholars, bishops and other leaders of religious thought were writing articles. One can also see from the names of those taking part in the agreed syllabus construction of those years, and, indeed, right back into the 1920s, that many prominent theologians felt a sense of involvement in and responsibility for religious education.[28] This is no longer the case today, and even when organising a consultation on a topic such as the teaching of the Bible in schools, it is not easy to discover theologians who are willing to take part.

Reasons for this rift are not difficult to suggest. In earlier decades there was a direct connection between theological studies and religious education, such that it was sufficient for a New Testament scholar to give a talk to a group of teachers on 'Recent developments in the study of the Fourth Gospel' for him or her to know that what was said would be of immediate relevance to the curriculum concerns of many of the teachers, particularly in the secondary school. In that sense, religious education was a sort of handmaiden of theology. It was taken for granted that religious education teachers were communicating to children what theologians were communicating in universities and seminaries to older students. Thus the emphasis was upon the similarity of the content of teaching religion in universities and schools. Although there was awareness of the problems created by presenting this material to younger pupils, these problems were not seen to be as complex as they are today, nor were there the problems of rationale created by philosophy of education for religious education. It looks as if the religious education ship has quietly slipped its moorings and sailed away into the high seas, with a crew of navigators and sailors quite different from those who guided the ship when it quietly navigated the internal canals of the domestic world of theological communications. Few theologians in Britain today appreciate the maturation in educational studies which has taken place since the Second World War and the complexity of the literature which has accompanied this. To comment usefully and knowledgeably upon trends in religious education requires some familiarity with some of the educational research literature, and when one remembers the comparable increase in technical sophistication of the theological literature which has also taken place, it is not surprising that few theologians have the surplus time, energy and motivation to undertake this interdisciplinary enquiry.

The word 'interdisciplinary' is itself significant. Religious education is a set of disciplines enclosed within a set of disciplines. Theology is also a set of disciplines. The problem of the relationships between these sets of disciplines is much more formidable than the situation which previously prevailed when religious education was a mere handmaiden of theology, or was conceived of as a matter of teaching theology at a simpler level and so primarily concerned with 'how to put it across'. Even today, one will occasionally encounter the view from a theologian that the task of theology teaching in universities is to equip would-be teachers with knowledge of their subject matter while the task of the teacher-trainer in religious education is to offer advice on how to communicate that content to children. This sharp distinction between content and context still persists with respect to religious education, although it sounds strange when coming from those who in other aspects of the work of theology today emphasise the need to contextualise the subject.

The increase in the complexity of religious education, and its dependence on an extensive educational research literature, no longer make it acceptable for the well-meaning theologian to write the occasional book and article about educational problems in which there will be no more than a reference or two to the educational and religious educational literature.

In other words, the relationship between theology and religious education is today more round-about and less direct. One has to approach religious education by way of educational studies. One does not come from theology to religious education by simplifying the content of theology, but by approaching religious education in its appropriate secular context and in order to (amongst other things) contribute towards a rationale for the subject. Thus we see that the relationship between theology and religious education is now part of the hermeneutics of the social sciences, in so far as education is a social science.

We may also notice that whereas in earlier decades religious education required theological support in the sense that it was dependent upon theology for its rationale and for the legitimisation of its content, the situation today is quite different. Religious education does not stand in any greater need of theological support than do educational studies as a whole. The support which theology might give to religious education would be simply an example of the support which it might offer to other aspects of education or to other social sciences. Thus there no longer need be a particularly intimate relationship between theology and religious education. The latter is just one of a large number of secular enterprises, including economics, politics, the arts and other cultural activities, which permit or attract theological comment. Although, on the whole, practitioners of these economic, political and social sciences and of the arts do not believe that their pursuits are deprived of legitimacy should they lack theological support, many who practise these disciplines are today increasingly ready to accept that theology may well have a role as an illuminating critic. This then is another possible reason for the rift between theology and religious education: not only has the relationship in itself become complex, but religious education is but one of a large number of contemporary social, professional and ethical questions which might attract the theologian's interest.

In spite of all these differences, the task is under way. F.H. Hilliard in his 1964 Hibbert Lecture[29] remarked that the rift between religion and education would not be closed until a theology emerged which was able to embrace the secularity of education. In the twenty years which have elapsed since then, we may believe that much important work has been done which should make for a happy and intimate relationship between these two great human concerns, allies for so many centuries, and alienated only temporarily in our time.

4 Concluding Observations

Reference was made in the opening paragraphs of this discussion to the possibility that the question we are addressing might be taken to mean that theology is or might be equivalent to religious education. Some theologians and some specialists in religious studies seem to agree, as we have seen in section 3 (page 44), that their academic pursuits, suitably simplified, could take the place of religious education in the curriculum. It is sometimes said that theology alone can determine how theology can be taught, or that how one is to learn from religious studies is a matter to be decided by religious studies alone. I have said more than enough to show how opposed to this idea I would be. Far from theology or religious studies providing the only norms for their own educational role in the schools, they cannot even exclusively provide such norms for their teaching work in universities and colleges. As long as such institutions are committed not only to research but also to teaching, and must thus be thought of as educational institutions, educational principles must play a part in the determination of what is to be taught. The teaching work of many university departments of theology might be considerably improved if it were more seriously thought of as providing for the religious education of intelligent young adults.

There is a much more interesting and profound interpretation of the question 'Can theology have an educational role?', an interpretation referred to in section 1 (page 40) as the third sense of the question. Two hundred or two hundred and fifty years ago a slow change began to take place in the way in which participation in the Christian faith was theologically expressed. Faith began to be seen as a modification of consciousness such that participation in Christianity could be conceived of as a learning experience. Christianity thus had an educational role in the growth and development of personality, indeed of culture and world history. Theology had an educational task in so far as it was the articulation of that learning experience. In the eighteenth century, a number of religious thinkers, both Jewish and Protestant, saw that if any religious truth is to be believed, then that religious truth must be received internally by the believing person, and must be integrated into the on-going pattern of that person's experience of life. It was seen that the nature of religious truth and of personality is such that if religious truths are received by a person in some other way (say on more authority, or because of tradition, or because of revelation conceived of as giving information external to the person), then any such religious ideas would not be truly religious, nor would they truly be ideas. In other words, the historical, social and personal contours of religious belief began to be perceived. This education or person-centred emphasis was expressed in the theology of Friedrich Schleiermacher in Germany, Samuel Taylor Coleridge in England and Horace Bushnell in the United States, to name the three countries principally represented in this volume. At the same time modern conceptions of education and the person began to appear in the work of educators such as Jean-Jacques Rousseau, Pestalozzi and Froebel, who were themselves all profoundly

influenced by religious ideals. So we may say that an educational view of
theology, a theological view of education, and a deeper understanding of
the nature of the human person, all three of these strands of thought
emerged in our Western culture more or less simultaneously, and relatively recently. The consequences for theology of this invasion by ideas
taken from education, learning and the nature of human development are
still very far from being properly understood. Historians of modern religious thought recognise that there has been a conflict between the claims
of theology and of science to express objective truths; it is perhaps less frequently recognised that there was an emerging alliance between subjective (personal) theology and subjective education which was providing
an alternative understanding of Christianity in opposition to the older,
external propositional form of theology which was now reckoned to be in
conflict with science. This 'educationalisation' of theology is often
described in histories of modern religious thought as being the development of an experiential theology (Schleiermacher), or a romantic theology
(Coleridge and Bushnell), or an existentialist theology (Kierkegaard), but
all these are nothing but specialised forms of the *educational* theology
which was emerging. A vivid example of this may be seen in the use of the
expression 'humanisation' in the educational theology of F. D. Maurice,[30]
and the history of the development of the doctrine of the atonement illustrates the same trend.[31]

It is out of such a pattern of educational and theological ideas that our
modern theories of Christian nurture and religious development of the
person have emerged. This also enables us to see how and why in British
religious education today an attempt is being made to conceive of some
way in which human development may be advanced by means of a learning encounter with religion, but in a form other than Christian nurture.[32]
In other words, the educationalising of theology has been the fore-runner
of the educationalising of religious instruction, and so this whole process
may be thought of as a particularly relevant example of the impact of theology upon religious education. But theology itself has not remained
unchanged by this contact with education. Theology is increasingly conceived of as having an educational task in a manner which would have
been abhorrent to Karl Barth[33] and his disciples. The dialogue can only go
on if there continues to be a further educationalisation of theology and a
further theologisation of education. One of the major tasks of the next few
years will be to determine the extent and benefits of this mutual inter-
penetration of theology and education, and to set up its limits.

Notes and References

1 For a discussion of some of the issues dealt with in this section, see my
   article 'Theology and religious education', in SUTCLIFFE, JOHN (ed.)
   (1984) *A Dictionary of Religious Education*. London: SCM Press.
2 MURPHY, JAMES (1971) *Church, State and Schools in Britain,
   1800-1970*. London: Routledge and Kegan Paul (58 f.)

3 BATES, DENIS J. (1976) 'The Nature and Place of Religions in English State Education, 1900–1944.' Unpublished Ph.D. thesis, University of Lancaster, chapter 4.

4 PAUL, AGNES S. (1919) *Some Christian Ideals in the Teaching Profession.* London: Student Christian Movement.

(1924) *Education, being the report presented to the Conference on Christian Politics, Economics and Citizenship at Birmingham, April 5–12, 1924,* Vol. II. London: Longmans, Green.

(1928) *Report of the Jerusalem meeting at the International Missionary Council 1928. Vol. II, Religious Education.* Oxford: Oxford University Press.

RAVEN, CHARLES (1928) *Christ in Modern Education.* London.

OLDHAM, J. H. (1931) *Christian Education, its Meaning and Mission.* London: The Auxiliary Movement.

YEAXLEE, BASIL (1931) *The Approach to Religious Education.* London: Student Christian Movement.

5 Chapter 2, 'Theology and Education', in (1970) *The Fourth R. The Report of the Commission on Religious Education in Schools.* London: SPCK, draws inferences for religious education from what might be called the general style of contemporary theology (paras. 110–16) and has one example of a theological assessment of an aspect of general educational theory (para. 129 ff.), but no attempt is made to trace the impact upon religious education of the theological trends between 1870 and 1960 (see paras. 69 and 80).

Patrick Miller's chapter, 'Recent trends in Christian theology', in SMART, NINIAN and HORDEN, DONALD (eds) (1975) *New Movements in Religious Education.* London: Temple Smith, while doing very well what it sets out to do, does not attempt to show any relationship between Christian theology and education.

6 COLERIDGE, SAMUEL TAYLOR (1830; reprinted 1972) *On the Constitution of Church and State.* London: Dent (Everyman's Library).

MAURICE, F. D. (1835) *Subscription no Bondage . . .* Oxford.

STYLER, W. E. (ed.) (1968) *Learning and Working: Six Lectures.* Oxford: Oxford University Press.

SOKOLOFF, M. B. (1973) 'Revelation as Education in the thought of F. D. Maurice.' Unpublished Ph.D. thesis, Columbia University, New York.

SADLER, JOHN H. (1983) 'The Contribution of William Temple to the development of English Education, 1905–1924.' Unpublished Ph.D. thesis, University of Birmingham.

7 MURPHY, J., op. cit. (see note 2).

CRUICKSHANK, M. (1963) *Church and State in English Education 1870 to the Present Day.* London: Macmillan.

STARKINGS, DENNIS (1980) 'Some Perspectives on the Settlement of Religious Education in England, 1944.' M.A. dissertation, University of London.

BRALEY, E. F. (1934) *The State and Religious Education.* London: SPCK.

8 STEPHENS, THOMAS (ed.) (1905) *The Child and Religion*. London. Chapter 6, 'The Religious Training of the Child in the Church of England', and chapter 7, 'The Religious Training of Children in the Free Church'.

9 GORDON, P. and WHITE, J. (1979) *Philosophers as Educational Reformers*. London: Routledge and Kegan Paul. Chapter 9, 'Religion, Idealism and Education'.

10 (1932) *Modern Tendencies in Religious Education, a short critical survey with some practical recommendations*. Report of Commission on Religious Education appointed by the Scottish Sunday School Union for Christian Education.

11 Although there was nothing as dramatic in British religious education as H. Shelton Smith's 1941 protest again Liberalism in his *Faith and Nurture*, all the Agreed Syllabuses of the 1940s and 1950s were influenced by neo-orthodoxy and 'Biblical Theology'.

12 STRAWSON, WILLIAM (1969) *Teachers and the New Theology*. London: Epworth Press.
    MATTHEWS, H. F. (1966) *Revolution in Religious Education*. London: Religious Education Press.

13 SMITH, J. W. D. (1969) *Religious Education in a Secular Setting*. London: SCM Press.

14 COX, EDWIN (1982) 'Educational religious education', in HULL, JOHN M. (ed.) (1982) *New Directions in Religious Education*. Brighton: Falmer Press (53–7).

15 MARVELL, JOHN (1982) 'Phenomenology and the future of religious education', in HULL, J. M., op. cit., pages 69–76.
    COX, EDWIN (1983) 'Understanding religion and religious understanding';
    OUELLET, FERNAND (1983) 'Religious understanding: an obsolete concept in the public school context?'; HANSEN, BENT SMIDT (1983) 'Phenomology of religion: a bridge between the scholarly study of religion and religious education': all *British Journal of Religious Education*, 6, 1, 3–19.

16 Some of the points may be observed in Paul Hirst's writings about education in the mid-1970s, e.g. (1974) *Moral Education in a Secular Society*. London: University of London Press Ltd.

17 DAVIES, RUPERT E. (1974) *A Christian Theology of Education*. Nutfield, Surrey: Denholm House Press; this may be considered as seeking to solve the problem created by the attempt to reconceptualise the task of theology as applying to secular education and not merely to Christian education within the churches.

18 See page 106 of my article 'Open minds and empty hearts?' in JACKSON, ROBERT (ed.) (1982) *Approaching World Religions*. London: Murray.

19 GOODERHAM, DAVID (1983) 'Dialogue and emancipation: new horizons in the development of religious education?' *British Journal of Religious Education*, 5, 2, 59–66.

20 CAPALDI, GERARD (1983) 'Christian faith and religious education: a

perspective from the theology of liberation'. *British Journal of Religious Education*, 6, 1, 31–40.

21 (1982) 'Religious education through story'. *British Journal of Religious Education*, 4, 3.

22 ZAKI, YAQUB (1982) 'The teaching of Islam in schools: a Muslim viewpoint.' *British Journal of Religious Education*, 5, 1, 33–38.

23 ANDREWS, MARGARET H. (1981) 'The Use of Metaphors as Models in Religious Discourse with Special Reference for implications for Syllabuses of Religious Education.' Unpublished M.Phil thesis, University of Aston in Birmingham.

24 SLEE, NICOLA (1983) 'Parable teaching: exploring new worlds'. *British Journal of Religious Education*, 5, 3, 134–8, 146.

25 TAYLOR, JOHN (1976) 'Initiation into agnosticism'. *Learning for Living*, 15, 4, 129–30.
NEWBIGIN, LESSLIE (1982) 'Teaching religion in a secular plural society', in HULL, J. M., op. cit., pages 97–107 (see note 14).

26 HARDY, DANIEL W. (1982) 'Truth in religious education: further reflections on the implication of pluralism', in HULL, J. M., op. cit., pages 109–18.

27 See the work of the Standing Conference on Inter-Faith Dialogue in Education, Friends House, Euston Road, London, NW1 2BJ.

28 The Committee of *The Cambridgeshire Syllabus of Religious Teaching for Schools* (1924) included Alexander Nairne, W. B. Selbie, T. R. Glover, Sydney Cave, Andersen Scott and W. R. Sorley.

29 HILLIARD, F. H. *et al.* (1966) *Christianity in Education*. London: Allen and Unwin.

30 SOKOLOFF, M. B., op. cit. (see note 6).

31 REARDEN, BERNARD (1971) *From Coleridge to Gore, a century of religious thought in Britain*. London: Longman.

32 GRIMMITT, M. (1982) 'World religions and personal development';
WEIGHTMAN, S. (1982) 'Realisation and religious education'; both in JACKSON, ROBERT (ed.) (1982) *Approaching World Religions*. London: Murray (130–60).

33 BARTH, KARL (trans. 1972) *Protestant Theology in the Nineteenth Century*. London: SCM Press.

Religious Education and Catechesis:

A Christian perspective on a necessary complementarity for a healthy society in a religiously pluralistic world

John H. Westerhoff III

Reflections on Work Done

I would like to begin with a few references to *Understanding Christian Nurture* (British Council of Churches, 1981). In that report the term 'Christian nurture' is used to denote that which occurs in churches and 'religious education' that which occurs in what are identified as 'secular schools'. The report established seven differences between them. Christian nurture, it is said, (1) has as its content Christian faith, (2) and as its aim the deepening of that faith. (3) As such it is a domestic activity of the church, (4) with a special paedological character (5) and appropriate only for Christians. (6) It assumes that both teacher and learner are *inside* the Christian faith, and (7) that it takes place within a worshipping faith community. With these criteria for Christian nurture I am in complete agreement, though I would prefer to name the phenomena *catechesis*.

However, when the report turns to similarities it names only one, 'critical openness'. Indeed, the first chapter is entitled 'Christian nurture in an open society'. In terms of similarities, I concur that 'critical openness' is a necessary criterion but I question whether or not it is sufficient. I wonder if the report is trying so hard to confront a closed-minded, uncritical, anti-rational, unhealthy understanding of religion and society that it unknowingly may fall into an alternative unhealthy understanding, namely one characterised by secularism, relativism, and rationalism. An open society prizes difference and diversity for their own sake and believes there is some rational means for mediating truth claims or establishing harmony. In order to overcome the negatives of a dogmatic heteronomous culture it adopts a relativistic antonomous one. A society founded on autonomy is destined to suffer from the pathology of anomie.

I would prefer therefore a pluralistic society and suggest that along with 'openness' a second necessary similarity to be recognised and affirmed is 'identity'. A pluralistic society is theonomous. It can be defined as 'a social order founded upon the principle of harmonious interaction for common ends among various distinct communities[1] each of which possesses both identity *and* openness. Such a society aims at enabling persons to say, 'aware of the numerous alternatives, I have freely chosen some particular faith which I will advocate by my words and example even as I remain open to others and maintain a critical stance both to my own and theirs.'

I maintain therefore that a healthy society in a religiously pluralistic world must be as concerned with identity as openness, and in that order. For unless a person knows who he or she is and feels good about that self, he or she cannot be truly open to others. Thus both religious education and catechesis must share a concern for both principles. Identity cannot be left solely to religious communities any more than openness can be left solely to the society and its schools. The principle of critical openness, as *Understanding Christian Nurture* rightly claims, is needed for a healthy community. But I would argue that the principle of identity maintenance is also needed for a healthy pluralistic society, and that the society and its schools need to provide religious education that supports both principles, though they will put their emphasis on openness and religious communities will put theirs on identity.

The rest of this essay will explore the nature and character of religious education and catechesis with special attention to both their differences and similarities in terms of a common commitment to the principles of identity and openness.

Definitions

RELIGIOUS EDUCATION Education is an intentional, valuable, long-lasting, interpersonal activity of the whole person which involves knowing and understanding in depth and breadth. The religious is concerned with the depth dimensions of life, people's ultimate concerns and commitments, and the search for the transcendent. In so far as any educational effort deals with patterns of belief or commitment concerning truth, goodness or beauty, it is religious. In one important sense, then, all education is religious. Similarly, a concern for the religious implies a critical examination of education. We need seriously and intellectually to explore the quality of life and the educational processes within our educational agencies and institutions. That which affects the human spirit, the sensibilities, the beliefs, attitudes and values of persons, cannot be ignored nor neglected. As the philosopher Alfred North Whitehead once wrote, 'the essence of all education is to be religious'. Further, the study of religion and the religious is a proper aspect of education. Our education is incomplete if we are not introduced to the literature, history, beliefs and practices of the world's various religions. Religion and the religious are important aspects of culture and every intelligent, well-educated person needs to be sympathetically and critically exposed to both the world's religions and the religious phenomenon. These two complementary concerns – the religious dimension of all education and education in religion – are the rightful and necessary concerns of religious education. Religious education properly addresses the questions: what does it mean to be religious and what does it mean to educate religiously? Religious education deliberately empowers people in their quest for relationship with the transcendent and enables people to give expression to this relationship. Thereby is the principle of religious identity supported. Religious education also deliberately helps persons to apply critical rationality to religion and the religious. Thus, the principle of critical openness is supported. Religious education, therefore, must strive for affirmative impartiality – that is, it shall never manifest agreement or disagreement with any religious tenet, nor manifest approval or disapproval of any religious practice.

Perhaps that helps to explain why religion and education have been married, divorced and remarried so often in their long history that it is easy to say that they cannot get along with each other any better than they can do without each other. Religion and education are destined to be a bickering couple who will never get along well when they are under the same roof, but who will be much worse off when they go entirely their separate ways. At the very heart of their uneasy relationship are inevitable strains and incompatibilities. Education must not resist the intrusion of religion just out of prejudice, and religion must not find the conditions imposed by education embarrassing merely out of a perverse arrogance.

There is a necessary dialectical relationship which needs to be established between the Christian community and its surrounding socio-cultural environment comprised of numerous religious and non-religious persons and groups. Christians need to regard the positive and enriching aspects of all other religions. We need to acquire an accurate understanding of our faith, religious experience and life in the light of others; we also need to develop an appreciation of others' insights and contributions to humanity and to promote joint efforts in the cause of a just and peaceful world. We need to do this, however, in ways that guard against the danger of religious indifferentism and relativism. Religious education when it is true to itself can provide a unique context for such efforts, providing it manifests the intention of striving to maintain both identity and openness.

To live with this parodox will not be easy. Identity necessitates subjective commitment, while openness necessitates objective critical reflection; identity requires complete participation, while openness requires observation. Religious education that maintains both principles does more than study the role of religion in culture, investigate objectively the sacred writings, beliefs, rituals and cultural products of religious communities, compare religions, or explore the religious phenomenon. It is not possible to understand the faith of others without participation in their worship and spiritual life. We cannot understand Buddhism without learning Buddhist forms of meditation. It is not possible to understand the sacred scriptures of a people solely through historical, literary and linguistic methods of investigation. We cannot understand the Bible without praying it. New methods will need to be developed for religious education if it is to be honest to both religious identity and critical openness.

Paul Tillich, in his essay 'A Theology of Education', differentiated between humanistic and inducting education. The humanistic ideal is the development of all human potential, individually and socially. Inducting education aims at incorporating persons into the life and spirit, symbols and traditions of a community. The two are different, and while they may be in conflict, they are not necessarily contradictory. If both maintain the principles of identity and openness they may be complementary. While the humanistic ideal will be the focus of religious education and induction the focus of catechesis, they will be able to support each other if they are able to express the paradoxical principles of identity and openness.

CHRISTIAN-JEWISH-MUSLIM-HUMANIST (AND OTHERS) EDUCATION There is good reason for all those engaged in the educational enterprise to explore their efforts from the perspective of their own particular religious faith. Education is best understood as all deliberate, systematic, and sustained efforts to transmit, evoke, or acquire knowledge, attitudes, values, skills or sensibilities, as well as any outcomes of these efforts. To think comprehensively about education we must consider a wide variety of agencies and institutions that educate, not only schools and colleges, but libraries, museums, day care centres, radio and television stations, government agencies, offices, factories, farms, voluntary associations and the like. Education must be looked at as a whole, across the entire life span and in all the contexts in which intentional learning occurs. All those persons – Christians, Jews, Muslims, Humanist and others – who engage in such efforts need to be aware of, and understand, the ways in which their faith (world view or value system) does and properly should relate to their efforts. A healthy society demands that persons be helped critically to examine their educational activities in the light of their religious convictions.

CHURCH, SYNAGOGUE (AND OTHER RELIGIOUS BODIES) EDUCATION Parochical (independent or private), as contrasted with state and non-parochial, schools have an important role to play in the education of the public. Special attention needs to be given to the unique and proper nature and purpose of these schools. While this concern, as well as that of the religious person involved in any educational effort, needs to be addressed, it is not within the scope of this paper to do so.

CATECHESIS Catechesis is community-centered activity; it depends on life in a community of faith continuously striving to mature in faith and live faithfully. Understanding catechesis as an aspect of ministry does not deny its educative character, it only chooses to see the educational elements as subservient to the ministerial. While catechesis is a particular aspect of ministry, it is comprehensive in that it relates to every aspect of the church's life. As such it aims to help the faithful, individually and corporately, to meet the twofold responsibilities which faith requires: community with God and community with all humanity. Catechesis aims to enable the faith community to live under the judgement and inspiration of the Gospel to the end that God's will is done and God's reign comes. Its content is not religion or the religious, but faith which is encompassed in the conviction that Jesus is Lord and life is lived under his Lordship. Catechesis asks, how do we make God's saving activity in Jesus Christ known, conscious, living and active in the lives of persons and the church? Thus it enquires: How is *faith* acquired, enhanced, and enlivened when faith is understood as perception? How is divine *revelation* made known when revelation is understood as a relational experience of God? How is our vocation realised when *vocation* is understood as sanctified individual and corporate human life? Translated into aims, catechesis strives (1) to sustain, deepen and transmit a Christian perception and understanding of life and our lives; (2) to aid persons to live individually and corporately in a conscious relationship with God; and (3) to enable persons to acknowledge and actualize their human potential for individual and corporate life. Having explored religious education in some depth I would like to do the same with catechesis.

Understanding Catechesis

Baptism tells us who and whose we are. Baptism establishes our identity by providing us with an image of who and whose we are and an image of the world as God intends it to be; it makes known our true selves in relationship with God and it establishes our vocation in the world. Throughout our lives we are called to live into that baptism. Herb Brokering, a Lutheran pastor friend, tells of visiting a Lutheran church near the Mexican border. When he arrived he was told that Israel (whose parents were Mexican) was to be baptized. Crossing the border to find a present for Israel, he fell in love with a pair of sandals. But they were for an adult and Israel was an infant. He tried to explain his problem to the saleswoman, but she said it didn't matter, Israel could grow into them. Israel slept through the ceremony, but his parents seemed to understand; baptism was a walk. A few months later he returned to learn that Lisa, Israel's cousin, was to be baptized. Back across the border he went in search of another present. This time he fell in love with a pair of bootees, only to learn they were for a two-month-old and Lisa was ten months old. He once again tried to explain the situation to the saleswoman, but she said that it wouldn't matter for Lisa could hang them on the wall to remind her of her baptism. At last, he said, he really understood baptism: it was living between bootees and sandals, between remembering and growing into, and all of us are on a pilgrimage with Lisa and Israel.

Catechesis is the process by which we prepare persons for their baptism and the process by which we aid persons to live into their baptism.

In the *Episcopal Book of Occasional Services* there is a rite for the 'Preparation of Adults for Holy Baptism' that is similar to the 'Rite of Christian Initiation of Adults' used in the Roman Catholic Church. Both the Roman and Episcopal churches have acknowledged the normative nature of adult baptism and Christian initiation. Normative means standard, rather than normal or typical, for in both traditions infant baptism continues to be affirmed and encouraged for the children of the faithful. However, by making mature adult baptism normative a number of important theological and catechetical convictions are communicated. First, Christian initiation involves both God's prior action and a human response. While God acts first, grace is prevenient, never acquired or earned by human effort but a gift, and while there are numerous appropriate ways for persons to respond over their lifetime, ultimately a mature, rational, moral response to God's ever-present transforming and forming love is normative for this conventional relationship to God. Second, baptism is a sacrament, not magic. A sacrament is an outward and visible sign of an inward and spiritual reality; it does not make something true, it only makes that which is already true, real. Baptism is not something we must do in order to convince God to give us salvation, it is what we do because we already know God's salvation. A child does not need to be baptized to acquire God's grace or be saved. Baptism is not a magical act that makes God do something for the person that God would not do without that act. Nor is it something which occurs without any human involvement. Sacraments are not encounters that 'give grace' but opportunities for those already in and aware of God's grace to celebrate that fact and thereby increase their awareness. And third, adult baptism asserts that importance of mature faith and life. While baptism makes known to us what is true, it assumes that we must always be living into, actualising, realising its truth. Thus baptism is the beginning of a journey for both infants and adults.

Nevertheless, by continuing to affirm infant baptism as a legitimate and laudatory exception to the standard, the church also teaches three other important truths about baptism. First, it establishes the fact that we are communal beings. Our faith is always someone else's faith first. We come to the church not primarily because we have faith, but because we want it. In the admission to the catechumenate in the *Book of Occasional Services* the priest asks, 'What do you seek?', and the catechumen replies 'Life in Christ', a life in the Body of Christ, the church, the community of faith. No one can be a Christian alone. To be a Christian is to live in a Christian faith community. Second, it is the faith of the church not the person that legitimises any baptism, whether the baptized is an adult or infant. For the church to baptize anyone, to adopt and induct them into the community, it needs to examine and reform its life as a faithful community. And third, a human being is always in process, that is, on a lifelong pilgrimage of daily conversions and nurture. Both transformation and formation are continuous aspects of human life. Catechesis implies more than conserving. Evangelization and catechesis belong together within the church. Evangelization is that continual process of renewal through daily conversions which provide the context for nurture. The fact of the church necessitates repentance understood as a continuous and lifelong process of transformations of our consciousness. It is not only the little wicket-gate through which John Bunyan's pilgrim quickly passes as he abandons the City of Destruction, but the entire pilgrimage to the Celestial City. Baptism is something we grow into as we are continuously converted day by day at ever deeper levels of our personality through the Word of God. Conversion proceeds layer by layer, relationship by relationship, here a little, there a little, until the whole personality has been recreated by God. Infant baptism makes clear this necessary lifelong process of living into our baptism.

In the new rubrics for catechesis in the *Episcopal Rite for the Christian Initiation of Adults* we also have some standards or norms established for the process of catechesis. But first, let me describe this recommended procedure and then draw out the implied principles.

Stage one is a pre-catechumenal period of inquiry, a time for evangelization. It suggests informal, natural settings in which lay persons share their life stories and what it has meant in their daily lives to have been baptized as a believer in Jesus Christ and incorporated into life in his church. It is a time for inquiries also to share their life stories and reveal what they are seeking. In a context of honest discussion, the Christian faith as a way of life in community will emerge. More important, an effort is to be made to help the inquirer to see where God's grace has been present in her or his life and how Christian faith and life in the church can help to make sense of this experience as well as give life meaning and direction. If any inquirer appears to desire 'life in Christ', the priest (pastor) needs to help candidates examine and test their motives in order that they may freely commit themselves to pursue the lengthy disciplined process of preparation necessary before baptism. If inquiries are deemed ready, a sponsor must be chosen from among the most faithful in the community to accompany them on their pilgrimage.

The next period, known as the catechumenate, begins with a public liturgical act at a Sunday Eucharist. At this time the catechumen and his or her sponsor begin a process which includes the following elements. First, the catechumen is to choose a ministry in which to engage. This ministry is not to be a service to the church, such as singing in the choir, but a ministry in the world such as service to the poor, hungry, sick, neglected, needy, or infirm. Second, with their sponsor catechumens are to attend regularly the Sunday liturgy and along with other catechumens explore how the story of their lives and the story of salvation celebrated in the liturgy intersect. Third, they are to gather regularly with their sponsor to develop a spiritual discipline for their life which includes learning to pray, meditate on Scripture, and discern God's will. During this period the candidate will be regularly examined and prayed for at the Sunday liturgy.

When it appears that the catechumen is ready, she or he is enrolled as a candidate for baptism (if the baptism is to be at the Vigil of Easter, this occurs on the first Sunday in Lent; if it is to be at the Feast of our Lord's Baptism, then it occurs on the first Sunday in Advent). During this period, amidst a number of important liturgical events, the candidate is encouraged to examine his or her conscience and to participate in the rite of reconciliation, to fast, to meditate on Scripture, and to pray in the context of directed retreats so as to test if he/she is spiritually and emotionally prepared. Candidates are also to reflect theologically on the Christian faith and life which they have been experiencing during this period of preparation. This important rational reflection on their participation in the life of the church provides an opportunity to reflect on Scripture, and to explore the church's fundamental theology and ethical norms to the end that they will understand and be able to defend both what Christians believe and how they are to live.

Then comes baptism (which properly incorporates baptism, confirmation and Eucharist in a single rite of initiation, and parenthetically establishes the standard of a single initiation rite for all those baptized, no matter what the age, as well as the standard of baptism as a covenant to be renewed over and over again in appropriate ways throughout one's life), but the process is not over. Following baptism, the newly baptized enter a final stage of catechesis. During the season of Eastertide or Epiphany they are helped to experience and reflect on the fullness of communal life in the church as a witnessing community in the world, and to acquire a deeper understanding of the meaning of the sacraments: baptism and Eucharist, the two great sacraments, and anointing, reconciliation, marriage, ordination and confirmation the other lesser sacraments. Thus the newly baptized learns that his or her growth and development have just begun and must continue through his or her life in the church.

PRINCIPLES FOR CATECHESIS From this recommended process a number of principles for catechesis can be established.

First, the process of catechesis is always related to evangelization and thus implies both a converting and nurturing process. It is concerned with a conserving need to form or shape persons in the tradition of the church and a transforming need to liberate persons from erroneous understandings and ways of life as well as reform church belief and practice. Catechesis implies a dialogue between the tradition and our life experience. It is first and foremost an adult activity and never solely or primarily for children.

Second, the process of catechesis is one of experience, reflection and action. Understood best in terms of a circle, it asserts that we act before we experience, we experience before we make sense. This is the truth that justifies an infant's participation in the Lord's Supper; similarly it encourages the church to provide an environment where children and adults can experience the Gospel, participate with others in living that Gospel in community and witnessing to it in the world, before talking about it.

Third, the process of catechesis is related to readiness and not time, to appropriateness and not a packaged programme. Different persons have different learning needs, various learning styles and different capacities for learning. Catechesis must be tailored to meet human need and potential, rather than trying to fit persons into pre-established programmes and organisations. Persons learn at different rates and bring their own varied experience with them. Readiness is the key, not the completion of a particular course of study.

Fourth, the end of catechesis is a life-style which includes our total being as thinking, feeling, willing persons. It is not solely a concern for believing certain doctrines (whether understood or not), for having particular religious experiences, or for willing to be a part of some particular denomination. A Christian life-style includes character, a sense of who we are and the necessary dispositions, attitudes, and values related to that identity, and conscience, an activity of the whole person making rational decisions as a believer in Jesus Christ and a member of his church as to what is a faithful act; and conduct, a life that others see as a sign and witness to the sovereignty of God.

Fifth, catechesis is a personal pilgrimage with companions in community. It is not a process of moulding individuals into some predetermined design, nor is it a process of simply aiding individuals to grow up according to some internal design. That is, it is not doing things to or for persons. It is, rather, a process of journeying with another person within a community, that is sharing life together over some route of travel. It is a communal act of doing something with someone. It assumes a searcher, a person who is willing to let *his/her* common life be a resource for the other, and the conviction that truth is revealed to both of them as they share in this mutual pilgrimage quest.

Our spiritual pilgrimage can best be understood in terms of three pathways or trails to God. Each trail leads to God and thus none is superior to the others. While the first path is a natural place to begin and therefore appears appropriate for children, each may be travelled at any time, in any order. Similarly we may return to any trail at will, and the third trail is interestingly one that integrates the other two. Since a pilgrimage is as much a concern for the process of travelling as it is about the end of the trip, it is beneficial to travel each route; indeed, something is missed if we limit ourselves to one trail, yet each still reaches the same goal or summit.

The first path I have named the *Affiliative-Experiencing Way*. On this slow, easy path the community focuses its concern on transmitting its story and thereby forms its identity and that of its members. Together persons seek to participate in experiences of life in a family-like caring, nurturing fellowship. Intuitive knowledge nurtured by participation in subjective aesthetic experiences and expressed through symbols, myths and rituals is needed. The authority of the community is trusted as together they aim to establish and conserve a sense of tradition. As they journey along they are dependent on others for guidance to learn what it means to be pilgrims.

The second path I have named the *Illuminative-Reflective Way*. On this somewhat difficult traverse over the rocks the community encourages persons to search out alternatives as there is no marked trail. In this difficult effort to make it over the cliffs the community discovers the meaning of trust and intimacy. The community supports each person as he or she assumes responsibility for his or her own life. Together they engage in critical thinking, quest after intellectual truth, and are nurtured through rational reflection on experience which is expressed through signs, concepts, and reflective actions. Together they seek to test by experience and reason the authority of the community and to live prophetically in a visionary community. As they journey along together, persons are encouraged to establish a sense of independence, to explore their own way and share their findings with the community.

The third path I have named the *Unitive-Integrating Way*. On this complex path persons move back and forth between the two previous ways and thereby create a new way. On this path they search to discern that to which they should give their life and how they are to live. They want to assume responsibility for community life as they combine intellectual and intuitive ways of knowing and find meaning in both contemplation and action. They reconcile the paradox of 'Catholic substance' and its conserving of the tradition, with a 'Protestant spirit' of prophetic judgement and retraditioning. No longer caught between believing there is *the* truth which their authority knows and there is no truth, which means that everyone believes what he or she likes, they become aware of pluralism's option, accept a truth for their life and, while advocating it, remain open to other possibilities. Thus, they seek to live an interdependent, apostolic life.

Obviously the community needs to provide guides and companions for each of these ways.

Sixth, catechesis asserts that this process is an activity of the whole community. Catechesis assumes a communal understanding of human nature and the necessity of a faithful community – that is, a community which shares a common memory and vision; a community conscious of its roots and commited to its vision of the future. Catechesis assumes a community with a common authority. It also assumes common rituals or repetitive symbolic actions expressive of the community's memory and vision.

And last, catechesis assumes a particular sort of common life together that is more like a family than a social institution or voluntary association. As such it is a faith family which focuses on every aspect of life: the religious, political, economic and social; it calls for the elimination of role-playing and the involvement of the total personality: it is never neutral to emotion, but involves life shared in the depths of joy and sorrow, pain and pleasure; it is a life regulated implicitly by custom and hence does not demand explicit by-laws; it is a community in which our obligations to each other include whatever love demands rather than a contract in which if the community does not act as I believe it should, I leave; and, lastly, it is a community in which our worth is not in what we contribute or how much we participate, but is a consequence of our being.

Each of us is of value, for each of us is in the image of God. None is of greater worth or value than any other.

Further implications should be obvious. We need to examine our common life and become more critical of every aspect of parish life. We need to establish the degree to which our life is an expression of culture and the degree to which it is faithful to the Gospel. We need to contemplate whether or not we have interpreted the Gospel through a cultural perceptual field, or whether the Gospel is providing us with a perceptional field necessary to transform the culture in which we live. Since catechesis includes processes of intentional enculturation and critical rational reflection, both experience and reflection must be taken seriously. In order for catechesis to be faithful the church must be a moral community of mature Christians seeking to provide for themselves and those they adopt into the family, whether adults or infants, a context in which the Gospel is experienced and reflected upon, that is an ever-reforming nurturing, caring community of faith and life.

Catechesis addresses the nature and character of these interactive, dialectical processes by which persons mature in the faith of the church as they live into their baptism within an intentional community of Christian faith which shares a common memory, vision, authority, rituals, and life – more like a nurturing caring family than a task-oriented, goal-oriented institution. To catechize is to participate with others in a shared lifelong pilgrimage of daily conversions and nurture within a story-formed sacramental community: that is, to be ever shaped by the Gospel tradition within a community which moves from experience to reflection to action day by day throughout our lifetime. To be a catechumen is to be a pilgrim; to be a catechist is to be a co-pilgrim, a compassionate companion and guide journeying with other pilgrims in community.

Thus, catechetics and catechesis address the ends and means of believing, being, and behaving in community. Understood best as a communal interactive process, catechesis can be defined as deliberate, systematic and sustained interpersonal helping relationships of acknowledged value which aid persons within a faith community to know God, live in relationship to God, and act with God in the world.

Catechesis aims to provide persons with a communal context for living into their baptism – that is, an environment for experiencing the ever converting and nurturing presence of Christ as they, day by day, in community, gather in the Lord's name to be confronted by God's Word, respond to the gift of faith, pray for the world and church, share God's peace, present the offerings and obligations of their life and labour, make thanksgiving of God's grace, break bread and share the gifts of God and are thereby nourished to love and serve the Lord. Catechesis aims to provide persons with a context for falling in love with Christ and thereby having their eyes and ears opened to perceive and hence experience personally the Gospel of God's kingdom; it further aims to provide a context for persons to live in a growing and developing relationship with Christ that they might be a sign of God's kingdom come; and last, it aims to provide a context for persons to reflect and act with Christ on behalf of

God's kingdom coming. To reach these ends, there is a need to maintain, conserve and transmit the Christian tradition (activities of identity forma- tion), but there is also a need to evaluate, change and reform (activities of critical openness). Catechesis must be understood in terms of both inten- tional enculturation and deliberate critical dialectical activity.

Religious education and catechesis, while different in aim and method, share a commitment to the principles of identity and openness. More important, they form a necessary dialectic in a religiously pluralistic world. One without the other would result in a less than healthy society. Together they can aid us in our quest for personal, faithful life and societal justice and peace.

Appendix I: Catechesis and Ministry

Since I first joined a theological faculty a decade ago, I have been troubled by the professional understanding of ministry which emerged in the church a quarter of a century ago and its resulting seminary curriculum. Caught between an understanding of profession as a response to a personal call from God along with a corresponding recognition of per- sonal charisma (a God-given grace) by the church, and a modern secular view of profession as the possession of specialised knowledge and skills, the clergy appeared to have moved uncritically into the mainstream of modern history. Indeed, today most clergy understand themselves as pro- fessionals and in the United States the Doctor of Ministry degree has formalised the credentialing process for the profession: ministry. Further, a specialised lay ministry, the professional Christian educator, emerged and resulted in a growing disinterest among both clergy and laity in the church's educational ministry. As one ordained to the ministerial priest- hood in the Episcopal Church and engaged in the formation of future clergy in a United Methodist Divinity School I have experienced the disease of these developments.

Faith is a gift of God; theology is a human work, a deliberate, rational, reflective activity. Theology literally means talking rationally about God; its goal is knowledge and understanding through a critical inquiry into the meaning of faith. As such it demands a patient, laborious and at times tedious engagement of the mind. To the limit of intellectual potential, every mature adult Christian is obliged to think theologically.

Once upon a time the processes of thinking theologically were divided into three levels of reflection and discourse known as fundamental, con- structive and practical theology.

FUNDAMENTAL THEOLOGY Sometimes known as dogmatic the- ology, fundamental theology operates on that foundational level of reflec- tion and discourse which provides us with an intellectual description, explication and justification for the Christian faith. As such, it provides an introduction to the idea of Christianity and answers the question what is a Christian. A fundamental theology, such as Karl Rahner's *The*

Foundations of Christian Faith, explores the Christian tradition as it is found in the teachings of the early church Fathers, especially as expressed in the established creeds of the universal church – the Apostles' and Nicene Creeds – and in the Word of God as conveyed in the Holy Scriptures. Thus all rational theological reflection is rooted and grounded upon God's revelation vouchsafed to humankind in the biblical witness and the teachings of the church. Through an exposition of this tradition fundamental theology is written.

Christians are not free to believe anything they like; Christian ministers and Christian churches are not free to preach or teach their private opinions. To be a mature Christian is to know and affirm the tradition once delivered to the Saints. One Christian is no Christian. Personal convictions do not make one a Christian. Christian existence presumes and implies an incorporation into a community and its tradition. Christian means a common life and a common belief. As St Vincent of Lerins said in a famous dictum, characteristic of the early church, 'We must hold what has been believed everywhere, always and by all.'

This tradition is centered in the Apostles' Creed, that 'rule of faith' into which we are initiated at our baptismal profession. And as St Irenaeus wrote, it is this rule of faith that must guide our reading and interpretation of the Scripture. The Bible is an essential aspect of the tradition into which we are baptized; it is the church's book. As such, the Bible is a sacred book addressed primarily to believers, but the book and the church cannot be separated. It is not a book for individuals to read and interpret as they will. As St Hilary of Poitiers said in the fifth century, 'Scripture is not in the reading, but in the understanding', and it is only in the church using its norm of the ancient creeds that scripture can be adequately understood or rightly interpreted. It is the responsibility of fundamental theology to engage in this activity and provide the community with the fundaments of its traditions stated in terms that can be comprehended in a particular time and place in history.

CONSTRUCTIVE THEOLOGY Sometimes known as systematic or problematic theology, constructive theology operates on a second level of reflection and discourse, providing the church with an intellectual interpretation of its tradition as it is expressed in its fundamental theology. As such, constructive theology helps to make sense of life in our day in the light of the church's tradition. A constructive theology, such as John Macquarrie's *Principles of Christian Theology*, explores systematically what it means for Christians to say 'I believe. .' in our day. The Christian tradition expressed in the creeds and grounded in God's Word needs to be understood in terms of particular historical, social, cultural settings. The Christian tradition needs to be appropriated and critically reinterpreted afresh in every generation so that it might answer the questions raised in its cultural setting as well as integrate and illumine the dimensions of modern experience.

PRACTICAL THEOLOGY While fundamental theology rationally

reflects on what it means to say Jesus is Lord, and constructive theology rationally reflects on how saying Jesus is Lord makes sense out of our life and lives in a particular social, historical, cultural setting, practical theology rationally reflects on what it means to live as a believer in Jesus Christ and a member of his church in our day. As such it continually moves back and forth between our life experience and activity and the church's fundamental and constructive theology with the aim of discerning how we are to live in community as a sign and a witness to the Church's faith.

As such, practical theology is comprised of five dimensions and while each is distinguishable, none is to be understood as separate from the others. Indeed, they are to be integrated, each with the others, for properly understood each is simply one doorway into a single whole. These five interrelated dimensions of practical theology are as follows: liturgical, moral, spiritual, pastoral and catechetical.

The liturgical dimension (life as sacrament) focuses on life in a worshipping community, that is, the community's cultic or ritual life, which includes all those repetitive symbolic actions expressive of the community's myth or sacred story. The moral dimension (life as seeking the good of others) focuses on life in an acting community, that is, on the community's ethical norms and how believers in Jesus Christ and members of his church make decisions on faithful actions in particular moral situations, including our personal and social activity in the political, social, and economic realms of life. The spiritual dimension (life as relationship) focuses on life in a praying community, that is, life in the spirit or how we are to live in relationship with God, including meditation, contemplation and acts of devotion. The pastoral dimension (life as caring) focuses on life in a caring community, that is, life as grieving with others, how we are to live in relationship with our neighbours, which include those healing, sustaining, guiding, reconciling ministries which express themselves in care for the sick, the needy, the poor, hungry, the lonely and the captive. The catechetical dimension (life as induction and reflective integration) focuses on life in a learning community, that is, formation or the processes by which we are initiated into the church and its tradition and the converting-nurturing processes and reflection by which we are aided to live into our baptism by making the church's faith more living, conscious and active, by deepening our relationship to God, and by realising our vocation.

Each of these dimensions of practical theology is related to and includes each of the others. The Sunday liturgy of the church combines spiritual, pastoral, moral and catechetical actions. The first part of the liturgy, the service of the Word, is intended as catechetical action. The prayers are a spiritual action, as is the reception of the sacrament. The reconciliation offered by confession and absolution, the kiss of peace, and, when offered, the healing provided through anointing are pastoral actions. The moral is addressed as the liturgy frames character and conscience and empowers the people to go forth to love and serve the Lord.

The spiritual dimension of practical theology includes not only participation in the Eucharist, but the daily liturgy of the hours; it pastorally offers the rite of reconciliation, it catechetically provides for spiritual direction and morally aids in discerning the will of God.

The pastoral dimension of practical theology includes liturgically the act of anointing for healing, spiritually the discernment of the gifts of the spirit, morally the prayers of intercession, and catechetically the preparing of persons to use their gifts and graces.

The moral dimension of practical theology includes liturgically the act of baptism which establishes our identity and character; pastorally it frees people to act in healthy ways, spiritually it provides persons with that relationship to God which is foundational to all moral action, and catechetically it helps persons to learn to make moral decisions.

The catechetical dimension which is the focus of this paper also relates to all the other dimensions of practical theology. It therefore cannot be understood as a special field of knowledge, ministerial discipline, or separate activity in the life of the church.

However, in our modern historical period in the United States, practical theology ceased to exist. Its five dimensions broke apart and were dispersed throughout the theological curriculum. Liturgical theology became among some preaching, among others technique for conducting worship and among still others an aspect of church history. Even in those divinity schools which keep the study of liturgics (typically understood as the history, theology, and practice of worship and/or preaching) in the curriculum, those which taught theory did not teach practice. Separate specialists in liturgics and homiletics were trained, and professional organisations and journals to support these specialised fields of knowledge and skill emerged. Pastoral theology became counselling and was typically modelled after secular psychology. The separate field of pastoral care and counselling developed its own training programme and certification system known as CPE or Clinical Pastoral Education. It trained its own specialists, offered its own degrees, had its own faculty, professional associations and journals. Catechetical theology became religious or Christian education and modelled itself after secular pedagogy. It too developed its own degree programme, the MRE (Moral and Religious Education), and a group of specialists, directors of religious education. The field even developed its own schools to train lay Christian educators. Along with this field of specialised knowledge and skills came the usual graduate programmes, degree, faculty, professional associations and journals. Spiritual theology was ignored in most seminaries, and within those in which it remained spirituality was turned into either technique or a course or two in the area of historical theology. Moral theology was consumed under systematic theology, creating a new field of theology and ethics. Finally another speciality was added. While it has had various names, its focus was organisation and administration. Concerned primarily with institutional survival, it included church management, evangelism understood as church growth, stewardship understood as church finance and so forth.

Thus ministerial studies, a conglomerate of sub-departments and specialties came into existence. More significant, perhaps, is the fact that these studies tended to focus on 'how-to' concerns, or the application of what was taught in the 'more important' and 'theoretical' areas of Biblical, historical and theological-ethical studies, each parenthetically separate from the others and also with their own professional associations, journals, degree programme and faculty. Thus a devastating separation errupted between theory and practice. Worst, ministerial studies tended to become devoid of theological foundations as well as spiritual and moral dimensions.

Regretfully, denominations and local congregations modelled themselves along similar lines, established organisational structures to correspond to these divisions of labour, and sometimes hired ordained ministers or professional lay persons to direct or engage in these specialised ministries. Hence, now we have committees for worship, education, pastoral care, evangelism, stewardship, administration, building and grounds, and social action in most parishes. Seminaries are organised, faculty hired and a curriculum provided which models this estrangement of specialised areas of knowledge and skill. Is it any wonder that the church lacks vitality, wholeness of life and faithfulness of mission and ministry? It is my contention that until we can re-establish the field of practical theology and equip both the laity and the clergy to engage in this integrating enterprise, the church will be devoid of an adequate means for being a responsive and responsible community of faith. The ministry of catechesis has a special responsibility in this reform.

Thus we reach the close of this exploration into religious education and catechesis. I have focused most of my comment on catechesis because I believe it has been neglected. Religious education needs to establish itself as a field of study within the university context while catechesis as a dimension of practical theology needs to establish itself as a field of study within the seminary. Similarly religious education is a proper concern of the state's schools and catechesis a proper concern of the church. While both must be concerned with identity and critical openness, catechesis in the church will make identity central and prior, while religious education in schools will make critical openness central and prior. Together they create a necessary dialectic in a religiously pluralistic world and make possible a healthy church and society.

Appendix II: Catechetics

THE CONTENT OF THE CHURCH'S CATECHECTICAL MINISTRY

How do we make God's saving activity known, living, conscious and active in the lives of persons and the church?

1 How is *faith* acquired, enhanced and enlivened when faith is understood as perception?

AIM: To acquire, sustain and deepen a Christian perception and understanding of life and our lives.

2 How is divine *revelation* made known when revelation is understood as the experience of God?

AIM: To aid persons to live individually and corporately in a conscious relationship with God.

3 How is our *vocation* realised when vocation is understood as sanctified or perfected individual and corporate human life?

AIM: To enable persons to acknowledge and actualise their human potential for individual and corporate life.

PHENOMENA	EXPRESSED THROUGH	MANIFESTED AS
FAITH as perception		
(intellectually)	Believing	Tradition
(attitudinally)	Trusting	Centredness
(behaviourally)	Worshipping	Ritual
REVELATION as experience		
(intellectually)	Narrating	Scripture
(attitudinally)	Anticipating	Prayer
(behaviourally)	Relating	Community
VOCATION as human life		
(intellectually)	Visioning	Principles and norms for human life
(attitudinally)	Loving	Sacrificial concern for the good of humanity
(behaviourally)	Reflective – acting	Daily individual and corporate life in the Spirit

OBJECTIVES RELATED TO CATECHETICAL AIMS

1 To possess a personal knowledge and understanding of God's revelation as contained in the Bible, and to be disposed and able to interpret both its meanings and implications for daily individual and social life.

To achieve this objective we need:

(a) To know the Biblical story of God's action in history as our story.

(b) To be involved in the critical interpretation of the Biblical story.

(c) To be engaged in reflection on personal and social life in the light of the Biblical story as well as meditation on the Biblical story to discern God's will for our lives.

2 To possess a personal knowledge and understanding of the Christian faith as expressed historically in the church's creeds, catechisms, and theological formulations, and be disposed and able to reflect theologically on contemporary life and history.

To achieve this objective we need:

    (a) To be provided with experiences in community which are consistent with Christian understandings of God, persons, and society.

    (b) To be introduced to the historic attempts of the people of God to express their faith and to engage in a critical evaluation of the tradition.

    (c) To be engaged in reflections on contemporary life in the light of the church's historical affirmations so as to aid us in expressing our faith in meaningful ways today.

3 To possess a personal knowledge and understanding of the Church's history and be disposed and able to interpret its relevance for daily individual and social life.

To achieve this objective we need:

    (a) To know the story of our foreparents' struggles to become a community of faith and to live faithfully in the world.

    (b) To be involved in a critical historical investigation of the faithfulness of the institutional church throughout its history.

    (c) To be engaged in reflection on our contemporary striving to be a responsible and responsive community of faith in the light of our history and to be involved in the continuing reform of the church.

4 To renounce evil, turn to Jesus Christ and accept him as Saviour, to put our whole trust in his grace and love, and promise to follow and obey him as Lord.

To achieve this objective we need:

    (a) To be introduced to a community of persons who live their lives as a renunciation of evil and an expression of commitment in Jesus Christ as Lord and Saviour.

    (b) To be confronted with a clear intellectual understanding of the Gospel.

    (c) To be provided with continuing opportunities to reaffirm the renunciation of evil and to renew commitment to Jesus Christ as Lord and Saviour.

5 To experience a personal relationship with God in Christ and to participate in God's continuing revelation.

To achieve this objective we need:

    (a) To have our intuitive mode of consciousness enhanced and to be inducted into life in a community of meditation, prayer and worship.

    (b) To explore rationally and critically the spiritual life.

    (c) To be aided in our spiritual pilgrimage through the development of a spiritual discipline.

6 To be a faithful and responsible member of the Christian community of faith and to share in its life and mission.

To achieve this objective we need:

    (a) To be offered experiences which enhance our sense of belonging to a loving, caring, affirming community of faith and to be aided in building a sense of trustful, responsible relationship with others and to be provided with opportunities for service in the church's life and mission.

(b) To engage persons in a critical exploration of the church's mission and ministry.

(c) To be engaged in meaningful and faithful participation in the church's mission and ministry.

7 To be aware of our Christian vocation and both be able to make moral decisions in the light of the Christian faith and be disposed to act faithfully and responsibly in daily individual and corporate life.

To achieve this objective we need:

(a) To be provided with experiences foundational to the formation of Christian character and be exposed to role models of the Christian life.

(b) To be aided in the development of Christian conscience and given opportunities critically to explore the application of Christian faith to individual and social life.

(c) To be enabled to act and reflect faithfully and responsibly in our daily individual and corporate lives, to the end that God's reign and God's will is done.

8 To understand and be committed to the church's corporate mission in the world for justice, liberation, whole community, peace and the self-development of all peoples, and be disposed and able to engage in the continual reformation of church and society.

To achieve this objective we need:

(a) To be introduced to a community of faith engaged in mission and be provided foundations for an awareness of corporate self-hood, justice, freedom, community and peace.

(b) To be given opportunity critically to explore the necessary reformation of church and society.

(c) To be equipped and motivated to engage in the reformation of the church and society on behalf of justice, liberation, whole community, peace, and the self-development of all people.

9 To possess an appreciative understanding of other faith traditions and to be able to enter into meaningful dialogue and action with them without sacrificing the integrity of one's own faith.

To achieve this objective we need:

(a) To be exposed to persons of other faith traditions and their understandings and ways.

(b) To be helped to explore intellectually and experimentally the faith of other persons.

(c) To be engaged in meaningful dialogue and actions with persons of other faiths.

A Response to John H. Westerhoff III

John Gibbs

There is much in Professor Westerhoff's paper with which I am in agreement. I have picked out three points in it for comment.

The paper begins with certain comments on the British Council of Churches' report *Understanding Christian Nurture*. The description of Christian nurture given in that report is accepted, but the title 'catechesis' is preferred. Professor Westerhoff, however, thinks the category of 'critical openness' used in the report is insufficient when considering the similarities between religious education and Christian nurture and suggests the category 'identity' as a necessary additional similarity. His criticism of the report here is that it appears to be confronting 'a closed-minded, uncritical, fundamentalist sectarian understanding of life and it falls into a secular, relativistic, liberal trap'.[1] An open society, he says, prizes difference and diversity for their own sakes, so he prefers the word 'pluralistic' to 'open'. It is not clear to me what he means by the statement that a pluralistic society is theonomous, but he defines it as 'a social order founded upon the principle of harmonious interaction for common ends among various distinct communities each of which possesses both identity and openness'.

Since I was chairman of the working party which produced the report, I am anxious not to appear too defensive about it, but I think there is an issue here which is more than semantic. The problem with religious education in England and Wales is more radical than Professor Westerhoff allows. The word 'pluralist' in his paper is used to denote a religious pluralism, as it appears in his subtitle. When he speaks of the necessary dialectical relationship between the Christian community and its surrounding social-cultural environment, he goes on to say that it is comprised of numerous religious and non-religious persons and groups, but nevertheless it is coherent religious groupings he appears to have in mind. What is meant in the report by an 'open society' is a secular society: that is, one in which no single view of man and society predominates, and therefore there is a necessary recognition of many views, religious and non-religious, competing for allegiance.

In Western Europe, the background of the debate on religious education today is that of a rapid movement from a society based on a Christendom model where there was little distinction between church and state to one in which religion is more and more marginal. In the former society, schools were regarded as agents of the church and that was still the assumption of the 1944 Education Act, whereas in today's pluralistic society schools must be (to use an unsatisfactory word) neutral in matters of faith. Christian nurture is no longer the task of our County schools.

This process, known as secularisation, is too well known to need rehearsing further, but I think it important to say that it is not necessarily anti-religious. In fact, a good case can be made out for the assertion that secularisation is a fruit of biblical religion and can be viewed as a religious achievement. It is therefore possible to have a Christian view of secular education, which in turn highlights the difference between it and Christian nurture.

The debate about religious education in County schools is about the justification of any religious education in schools, and, if it can be justified, then it is about the aims and content of such religious education. In this debate the most common charge against religious education in schools is that it is a process of indoctrination, so there is some justification in Professor Westerhoff's observation about the report appearing to confront a closed-minded fundamentalist sectarian understanding of life, because religious education in schools is commonly lumped together with an authoritarian sect-like mentality and written off on educational grounds. So there is an important area of discussion about the place of religion in the school syllabus, and if it can be justified (as I believe it can), then it must be on educational and not primarily on theological grounds.

I take what Professor Westerhoff says about the dangers of religious indifferentism and relativism, and I am grateful for the clear description of the paradox with which we must live. Yet it seems to me that it is *identity* which is the real casualty in the process of secularisation, and that is why the problem is deeper than I think he allows.

Secular education is critical, open, person-centred, and always committed to the spirit of enquiry. It cannot be neutral since it has to decide what is worthy of enquiry, but it demands objective, critical reflection. Christian nurture shares much with secular education, but it is less open about the future. As the British Council of Churches said in an earlier report (*The Child in the Church*, 1976), 'Secular education fails if it produces a bigot but not if it produces an atheist. Christian nurture fails if it produces a bigot and an atheist.' Christian nurture is more specific about a Christian future and occupies a middle position between closed authoritarian structures and open enquiring education.

I remember being stung by some words of Professor David Martin,

'. . . the end of religion (in schools) is not free secularity but political myth', and for many Christian teachers in our schools the problem is compounded by the thought that to give up what has been a privileged position in religious education might mean making way, not for open debate and enquiry (which is a proper educational aim), but for indoctrination in other viewpoints inimical both to our cultural traditions and to Christian truth.

What is certainly true (and here I agree wholeheartedly with Professor Westerhoff) is that the task of Christian nurture is now in no uncertain manner laid upon the churches, and as far as the Church of England is concerned it is ill-equipped for the task.

The second point I have selected for comment is Professor Westerhoff's consideration of baptism and Christian nurture, and especially the implications of his phrase 'catechesis is the process by which we prepare persons for their baptism and the process by which we aid persons to live into their baptism'. I am reminded of some words of a former colleague: 'Whereas parents in the early Church were so clear about the meaning of their baptism that they demanded baptismal status for their children, we have acquiesced in the continuance of infant baptism while being utterly vague about what baptismal status implies.'

I am not sure about Professor Westerhoff's phrase used in relation to infant baptism, 'a legitimate and laudatory exception to the standard', but I agree with the three truths about such practice, namely that it is communal (that is, into a community), that it is into the faith of that community, and that it is into a process of growth. Nurture is indivisible. May I enlarge on this (which I am sure will not be in contradiction to Professor Westerhoff's paper).

Within the church in the United Kingdom we are still dominated by nineteenth-century views of education in our approach to children and educational methods. In both popular and independent educational traditions great emphasis was placed upon social objectives: moulding children for their eventual place in society. This community emphasis accounts for the common view of the church that a child is a potential adult: that is, someone on the way to faith, a potential member of the church community. Nurture therefore is about something in the future, and the child has to break into the adult world. Baptism, however, is about *present* membership of the church and should inaugurate a steady, continuous and natural growth in faith. A crash course for confirmation preparation, as one finds in many churches, is hardly adequate nurture. Our failure is often a failure to take seriously the *present* needs of children and minister adequately to them, and it is not without significance that we speak of instructing, training and educating children, but rarely about a ministry to children. Childhood is a lively subject in many fields of study, but the theologian has little, if anything, to say. What is a child? What are his or her needs? What is his or her relationship with the living God? What is his or her actual initiation into the life of grace other than our instruction about it? What can he or she teach *us* about the Christian life? The structuring of experience for the child to explore is the process of religious education, but it is the illumination of those experiences into an awareness of God's presence which is true religious growth. That is not something in the future but in the present, and we need a Christian view of childhood for an understanding of nurture.

We also need a new understanding of the local church as a community of growth. The church itself is the agent of nurture. To say that the Christian life is one of continuous growth is one of those truisms with which nobody will disagree. We all believe it, but there are all too few Christian communities which order their life to give it effect. It is only as we can experience love, compassion, forgiveness (and other religious qualities) that they can be understood, and it is by living within a community which embodies them that nurture takes place. The church is not just a convenient organisation for propagating the Christian faith; it is the realisation of that faith and the place of Christian nurture.

The third point I have chosen for comment is Professor Westerhoff's section on 'Catechesis and Ministry'. There is so much to agree with in this section, especially that part dealing with ordination training.

In the English scene, the role of the Anglican clergy has been shaped by particular developments in English society, and especially by the professionalisation of the clergy in the eighteenth and nineteenth centuries. The clerical role in the Church of England is still seen for the most part as that of the nineteenth-century professional man.

> In the dramatically altered social circumstances of the last quarter of the twentieth century the Church (i.e. the Church of England) is being called to re-examine the vehicle of its priestly ministry and to discover whether there is not much in the received pattern which, having been taken for granted for so long, merely serves to reinforce the marginality of the contemporary Church. For it is ironic that a part of the reason that the Church is now less able to exercise the priesthood of Christ in English society is because its own ministry has become trapped in an increasingly problematic institutional form.[2]

While sharing Professor Westerhoff's concern about the study of theology, I wish to add another consideration to his analysis. There is an interdependence between changes in contemporary society and changes in the structures of church life. This is because, in theological terms, the world is the locus of the Gospel. One of the difficulties facing the church today is that it is seeking to relate to a pattern of society which is fast disappearing and a pattern of life and organisation shaped by the needs of that former society. What is the task of the church in a pluralist society? It can no longer see itself as 'the cement' of society, and it lacks a clear understanding of the society to which it must now relate. In the privatisation of religion there are strong temptations to sectarianism: that is, for the church to confine itself to religious activities with which it feels safe – ritual, matters of belief, church practice, the interior life. If the church is not to withdraw from society, but to persist in working with the assumptions underlying its mission, then it must grapple with its own self-understanding in relation to contemporary society.

Today that relationship of church and world must be forged principally by its lay members and not, as in the past, by the clergy, and it is not without significance that we in the Church of England are rediscovering the New Testament note of shared ministry. Ministry belongs to the whole church and not just to an order within it, and the differentiation of function takes place within this understanding of the wholeness of ministry in which every member of the church shares by virtue of baptism.

The two pertinent questions then raised are, first, whether the nurture offered to members for their tasks is adequate, and second, what in this context is the clerical role? I will say no more about the first, but will finish with a comment on the second.

As far as ordained ministry is concerned (and I can only speak about the Church of England), I want to make the simple point that the clerical role must be much more of an educational and theological role than it has been. The priest must be the focus of Christian tradition for his people, enabling them in turn to undertake their tasks in the world; and that in turn means that the pattern of church life must be determined by the needs of its members.

As for training, I agree entirely with Professor Westerhoff that the great need is for ministers to think theologically. To my mind, that is the crunch of ordination training. It is not just about the accumulation of academic theological knowledge, but about the ability to put such knowledge to work, to think theologically about all tasks. It is about 'doing' theology rather than just learning theology. Clearly that includes all the points listed by Professor Westerhoff under his heading of practical theology. They are integrated by means of Christian theological reflection, which in turn enables these tasks adequately to be performed. Ministers are the resource people: teachers, enablers, illuminators, pastors, all engaged in the work of training and equipping the church for its mission.

References

1 A phrase used by Professor Westerhoff in his original draft but subsequently revised – *Editor.*
2 RUSSELL, ANTHONY (1980) *The Clerical Profession.* London: SPCK.

The Legitimacy of Religious Education in Secular Institutions

Howard W. Marratt

The title of this paper poses considerable problems for the lecturer: the possibility of overlap with other papers; the need for assumptions, if he is to be both brief and comprehensive; the diversity in background and attitude of his audience. It was tempting to proceed by providing a linguistic and conceptual analysis of the title's three nouns (legitimacy, education and institutions) and two adjectives (religious and secular), but the precedents from those who have thus approached a paper on 'religious education' are not encouraging. The reason is probably that an agreed understanding of the parts does not necessarily lead to an agreed understanding of the whole – as can be clearly seen by applying the description of 'Christian commitment' to both Mother Teresa and the Revd Ian Paisley. Nevertheless the title requires one general assumption – that it is improper for religious education in a County school in England and Wales (or anywhere else) to aim at achieving a particular commitment to religion, or, one might say, a commitment to a particular religion. If that be the unargued premise of this paper, some preliminary clarification of 'secular institutions' is necessary.

Schooling and Religious Education

With regard to 'institutions', this paper concentrates on primary and secondary schools (with obvious implications for those higher education institutions which provide undergraduate or postgraduate courses for teachers of religious education in schools). Religious Studies (or even Theology) courses in universities and other tertiary institutions have been treated by tutors as academic studies in their own right, with the result that these tutors have not regarded it as their duty, any more than lecturers in other subjects, to be involved in the personal (including, in their case, the religious) education of the student as a necessary part of his/her course. It is, however, important to note that during the 1960s expansion of teacher training in the United Kingdom both the Department of Education and the Area Training Organisations were increasingly concerned about that aspect of professional education usually described as the 'personal education of the student'. Not merely denominational but all county colleges of education felt a responsibility at that stage, especially in the field of moral education, to help students understand at their own level the issues which they would face in the classroom. Since such students include all primary school teachers as well as secondary non-specialist Religious Education teachers, it is a continuing responsibility of all institutions of teacher training to be concerned for the education of the whole student, especially as his or her attitude and personality in the classroom may be more effective than his or her subject teaching. The organisations which validate courses of teacher education in tertiary institutions have a clear obligation to ensure that this aspect of such courses is properly covered – though the fact that denominational colleges of education train teachers for both church and County schools further complicates their responsibility for this aspect of training.

The same responsibility for the education of the whole person is equally relevant for County schools. Although this paper concentrates on that part of the institutions where specific religious education is provided, religious education in some sense may be seen as a cross-curriculum and implicit activity of the whole school. Apart from school assembly (and whatever may be legitimate within it), the life, organisation and activities of the whole school community, as well as the attitudes and methods of all teachers, inevitably reflect and inculcate values, principles and a philosophy of life. Such implicit religious education may, consciously or unconsciously, be part of the total educational experience of the child and far more effective than explicit classroom religious education; the arguments which legitimate the explicit may be equally valid for the implicit, but what if there is a conflict in approach and intention between the explicit religious education lessons and the implicit activity of the whole school community? And who legitimates the latter?

Another limitation of this paper will be the application of its language and argument to secondary rather than primary schooling. Although it may be easier to justify religious education in institutions where pupils are on the threshold of reasoning and conceptual analysis, the principles of this paper apply throughout the whole school range, including the years when the non-cognitive and affective elements are more evident in the classroom and the role of the teacher appears more influential. Indeed, the very fact that primary institutions deal with pupils who are at a formative stage of development in religious and moral education, and who are more susceptible to indoctrination, usually ensures that primary school staff are sensitive to the dangers of their responsibilities and to the consequences of implicit education.

Finally, it is sometimes argued that a school institution should not be concerned with commitment, either in the pupils or in its own general stance. But since schools by their very nature prepare pupils for commitments of various kinds, it is surely important for them to induct pupils into the nature and implications of commitment. It is clear that even a school which attempts to adopt a neutral stance about issues such as religious education is itself a committed institution. It is all the more important, therefore, that schools should enable pupils to understand what is the nature and status of commitment and should ensure that the implicit and explicit, curricular and extra-curricular, activities of the school conform to such an educationally acceptable understanding.

Defining Secularity

With regard to the 'secularity' of such institutions, one becomes aware of the different pre-suppositions of terminology which bedevil debates in religious education, as well as of the weight of historical heritage which causes proponents and opponents to rationalize repeatedly in their desire to perpetuate, or react against, that heritage. The definition of 'secular' is, therefore, crucial for this paper. If it describes those institutions which are not founded or controlled by non-secular (usually religious) bodies and do not aim to educate pupils or students into a particular religious commitment, there will be no problem, for few, if any, religious educators expect secular institutions to 'make' pupils religious in a particular sense. But if 'secular' institutions signify an education which is irreligious or value-free and intended to 'make' neutral pupils, then there are two serious objections: first, because, under this definition, 'secular' assumes a definite ideological and quasi-religious stance, which is far from neutral; secondly, because schools cannot be divorced from the society which controls them, and most Western democracies are certainly not secular in this sense. The first objection is the more serious and fundamental, because, as most philosophers of education have argued, education itself is an ethical activity and all knowing leads to a process of evaluation and commitment. A secular institution, which excludes religious education is not neutral, but is either anti-religious or regards religion as unimportant; whether secular institutions can exclude religious education, as distinct from education in religion, on purely educational grounds will depend on our definition of both education and religious education.

Certainly the State – or, more accurately, the County (as distinct from the private) – educational system of England and Wales has been characterised by Christian views of man and his education; and since 1870 Free Churchmen, particularly, have given their support to Education Acts which enshrine an ideology broadly consonant with religious principles and to schools which may engage in secular activities but which are certainly not dominated by a philosophy of secularism – indeed, they expect those schools to reflect certain fundamental values and attitudes.

As for the social reasons for doubting the accuracy of 'secular' as a description of schools, we must admit the complexity of the situation. As far as the United Kingdom is concerned, religious organisations have played a large part in education and have influenced the contents of various Education Acts; but this in itself is no reason to justify the position in County schools. Furthermore, it is dangerous to proceed from the fact that the culture of any society is reflected in its educational system to the instrumental and functional argument that education must necessarily be a means of cultural transmission and all its contents be justified on those grounds; schools must induct pupils into their past, but not in such a way that they attempt to predetermine and condition their future. When one turns to societies such as the United States, however, the secular institutions include in their educational programme the moral and social norms of society, but not the religious stances. On closer examination, societies which exclude religious education from the curriculum (just as perhaps, in the past, those which included it) do so for historical rather than educational reasons. How long can any society continue to allow its educational system to be dominated merely by historical – or even cultural – arguments which may be out of date? Equally, it must be chary of denying its approval for merely transient cultural reasons.

It is surely time in the latter half of the twentieth century to move away from an education which not merely reflects (as is proper) the history and culture of a society, but also is totally dominated by it. It is the argument of this paper that, as far as the United Kingdom is concerned, the secularity of our society (and, therefore, of its schools), is such that it includes a plurality of religions, even though there might be a dominance of one; and that one of the greatest social reasons for the exclusion of religious education from secular schools, namely the bigotry and divisiveness of denominations and religions, is not, largely because of theological and inter-faith dialogue, a factor which is relevant in the United Kingdom, and ought not to be a factor in any society's schools. To define secularity in non-religious terms is to do a grave educational disservice to pupils, just as it is an insult to teachers to expect impartiality (as distinct from neutrality) only from those without convictions. The autonomy of the pupil is just as much at risk in a secular school as in a school of a religious foundation, if the former assumes, but never publicly defines, its secularity in terms of religious neutrality or so-called objective openness; in this case secularity has drifted into secularism. That is one reason for appreciating recent legislation which requires every County school in England and Wales to set out in writing its aims for the school as a whole and for individual pupils, and regularly to assess how far its curriculum measures up to these aims. How then will County schools legitimate their religious education?

Justifying Religious Education

In practice, of course, it is neither the philosopher of education nor the expert in curriculum development who legitimates religious education, but society, whose consensus is reflected in national legislation on the matter. For primary and secondary schools in England and Wales, although there may be local and national consultation, it is the Secretaries of State who are required 'to take an overall view of the content and quality of education' which will enable local authorities and schools to shape the curriculum in the light of national policies and national needs. Within such a national policy (in harmony, of course, with the 1944 and earlier legislations) one aim is 'to instil respect for religious and moral values, and tolerance of other races, religions and ways of life'; religious education, moreover, not only contributes to other aspects of the curriculum (for example, personal and social development) but also makes a distinctive contribution by providing 'an introduction to the religious and spiritual areas of experience and particularly to the Christian tradition which has profoundly affected our culture' (*The School Curriculum*, Department of Education and Science, March 1981, paras. 7, 11, 27).

Although the cynic might argue, as we have already noted, that such legitimacy is merely a cultural hangover, education cannot be divorced from its social context – past, present or future – not even for Plato's guardians. The philosopher of education must, therefore, face the claim that 'what is taught in schools, and the way it is taught, must appropriately reflect the fundamental values in our society' (op. cit., para. 21). This is not to imply that education is static in concept and functional in status or application, nor to make society rather than educational principles determinative. It merely signifies that dynamic educational development is only effective in a democracy if it takes account of the social context; students of the history of religion have long accepted the social factor in the emergence of a truth (or in a changed perception of the truth) and students of religious education must do the same.

There are, however, other bodies who legitimate education, including religious education. Validators of courses in tertiary and secondary education – the Universities, CNAA, GCE and CSE Boards, for example – not only approve the content of examination courses but also directly affect what is taught and the way in which it is taught in secondary schools in and below the examination years, and indirectly in primary schools. Not only is the legitimating process affected positively or negatively by the university don, the employer and the parent, but increasingly by the examination boards (particularly in the proposed 16 + criteria) which may have a significant effect not just on the content but on the philosophy, rationale and objectives of each subject.

There is no doubt that Parliament and the public, though they are becoming more aware of the distinction between moral and religious education, also expect religious education to contribute to moral education and to multi-cultural education. The consequence is that, while there may be justifications for ethical behaviour other than on religious grounds, and while some of the older methods of moral education were educationally indefensible, schools are expected to encourage (rather than 'instil' – the word used in *The School Curriculum*) moral attitudes and behaviour and not to be neutral when pupils behave otherwise; the moral aspects of religious education, therefore, will be regarded as educationally legitimate, provided that the methods satisfy educational criteria.

But if the legitimacy of religious education, in part or *in toto*, depends on the satisfaction of educational criteria – and no religious educator would wish otherwise – who decides upon such criteria within any society? Some philosophers of education have argued that education itself is an autonomous form of knowledge based on rational principles, which should determine the whole curriculum. Others regard education as a field of knowledge, or a corpus of activities, or as a process. Religious education may be regarded as non-legitimate either because it is not consonant with the definition of education or because its nature and purpose is misunderstood or misrepresented so that the stereotype (often a product of the critic's childhood experience as a pupil) is rejected by the educational philosopher. We must turn, therefore, from asking who legitimates religious education to considering what makes it legitimate, but in order to do so we must define the nature of education.

The Contribution of Religious Education

It is the argument of this paper that education is a cluster or complex of disciplines united by certain common principles and procedures (for example those of rational discourse) and by a concern for the development of the whole person – individually in his autonomy, socially in his relationships and purposefully in his future – taking account of his varied needs, intellectual, emotional, moral, physical, spiritual and so on. Though each discipline may contribute its special emphasis and distinctive procedures, its place within the whole depends on its ability to accept both the common principles and the concern for the development of the person. Although, therefore, the development of faith is fundamental, in religion, for the whole person, yet in a secular institution it would be excluded on two grounds: first, because the school is non-religious (in the narrow sense) in its objective; and secondly, because the procedures of faith (in the narrow sense) go beyond the common principles and procedures of the school.

But what kind of religious education would be legitimate within such a school? Again it is the assumption of this paper that religious education is concerned with the development of religious and spiritual understanding and insight. Although one may reject the definition of secularity as neutrality (preferring the notion of plurality of some kind), surely a secular school (which is non-religious or even neutral), sharing the two educational objectives and characteristics listed in the previous paragraph, must consider it legitimate to include the development of religious understanding within its curriculum; but, before doing so, it may wish to be assured that 'religious' is defined broadly (to include a variety of stances), for even agnostics and atheists will stress the importance of the religious' or the 'spiritual' (while rejecting the narrower overtones of the noun 'religion'); it will also want to ensure that the religious educator does not see his work as an extension of the church, synagogue, mosque, or temple and as designed to save his pupils from secularism.

The basis of such religious understanding will be a study of religion(s) and of what religious people believe and do (in rites and observances, as well as in the moral and social application of their beliefs). Such a field of knowledge is an essential part of an educated person's development. Admittedly there may be problems with the study of religion(s); the lack of time for more than a 'Cook's tour' (over against the basis of a more selective approach); the absence of a common terminology (or the use of the same word – soul, say – for quite different concepts); the danger of stereotypes or the treatment of a religion monolithically; the approach to be adopted (historical, sociological, anthropological, thematic and so on); the inadequacy of a merely phenomenological approach. All these difficulties justify the increasing emphasis on viewing the religion from the point of view of the believer, so that the pupils gain some feeling from the inside – a technique long practised in arts, literature and music, but now readily used in history and environmental studies. In this way, the pupil is not merely inducted into knowledge but also into understanding what motivates others at the depths of their being, including the religious, as compared with the economic or social, reasons for the actions of men in history. But such religious education could still be described as 'religious studies' for it might be no more than education into knowledge about religion. (And it could still be indoctrinatory; for, although the inclusion of more than one religion, and the re-definition of religion to allow for 'life-stances' such as Humanism or Marxism, might counter the charge of indoctrination, it is just as possible for a comprehensive religious syllabus to be undermined by biased methodologies as it is for a single religion to be treated in an open and critical manner such as may lead either to its acceptance or rejection; critics of religious syllabuses must look at methods as much as contents.) If the goal of religious education is to produce rational, autonomous persons, then the study of, or knowledge about, religion(s) is the only possible form of religious education which will satisfy the objectives of a secular school with this educational goal.

There is, however, a further aspect of this understanding which might or might not be regarded as acceptable, namely an understanding of the 'science' of religious study. The traditional disciplines within Christian theological study are an important part of a knowledge of Christianity – for example, in one area alone, the academic skills of biblical criticism, hermeneutics, linguistic analysis and epistemology (which should be part of the teacher's equipment and reflected in his or her approach to sacred scriptures in the classroom) will be part of education in rational autonomy, but they will also shield pupils from fanatical biblicism, even while making them aware and respectful of those who reach conservative conclusions within such scholarship. It is important to realise that the contribution of education 'in' (the procedures of) a subject to education 'about' that subject is not peculiar to religion; it is shared by most other subjects, not least history and science, which have in recent years joined art and literature and music in stressing, and even focusing the curriculum upon, the skills needed to 'do' history and science, rather than so much on the body of knowledge. (Indeed the Royal Society's 1983 report on science education goes further and speaks of education not only 'about' and 'in' science but also 'through' science, because it regards the moral and social implications of science as part of a proper scientific education.) Furthermore, it is significant that all subjects are beginning to appreciate not only the common rational approach to study which they may share, but also the variety of skills or procedures which contribute to education in a subject, some of which were previously not regarded as part of the discipline of that subject. For example, mathematicians and scientists increasingly stress the role of personal imagination in the development of concepts and hypotheses, which may not easily be susceptible to falsification criteria (apart from the fact that theories which satisfactorily met such criteria one year may, with new knowledge and procedures, be abandoned a few years later). This dynamic view of education will indicate to pupils that no subject is a monolith but that all subjects, from art and language to geography and physics, will use a variety of models to develop understanding of their insights; in such a way science, for example, may be prevented from descending into scientism, as much as religion into religiosity or superstition; and in such a way, too, will the form of statements in the classroom cease to be treated as immutable absolutes. Religious education, therefore, which involves the use of skills and models similar to other subjects, can surely share their legitimacy – though, like them, it must be wary that this approach does not become a rationalised functionalism.

The commonality and variety of educational procedures which legitimate aspects of the curriculum, if the pupil is to have a full and proper education, is paralleled by the diversity of the body of knowledge within each subject: the approach of natural science is broken down into the diverse activities of biologist, chemist and physicist (with the subjects, which, for example, almost undermine the concept of any one science and leave us with different types of biologist and so on); the historian must take account of different complementary, even contradictory, interpretations of events in one country or epoch, as well as the history of different countries or epochs. In this way the scientist or the historian may avoid the charge of indoctrination – for example, always studying British history, or inducting pupils into a merely European viewpoint. Similarly, the study and understanding of religions is included in the curriculum of religious education, not primarily for instrumental reasons (to understand immigrants of other cultures, or to become an informed traveller on business or pleasure or an educated world politician), but because there are various and diverse (and in some respects totally contradictory) approaches to the nature of existence and of humankind, amongst the religions. A full education in a secular institution must allow pupils to be introduced to this diversity. The problem for the educator in religion, as in history, for example, is to adjust the selection of material to the time available; and it is at this point that the educator faces the problem of the criteria for selection, since overall coverage is quite impossible. In whatever ways the historian may attempt to solve his (her) problem (and in some senses, if he (she) is committed to one ideological standpoint, the problem is very similar), the religious educator, especially in a secular institution, is faced with an additional peculiar difficulty: each religion is autonomous and claims an authority from outside; any attempt to provide a comparison or synthesis between religions is beyond the scope of education at this level, would be unjust to each religion, and would consciously or unconsciously promote the view that there was a superior, objective, stance of religious plurality, or syncretism, or neutrality, which was preferable to any commitment to one particular religion. The general problem of representative selectivity (shared by historian and religious educator) and the particular problems of religious authority are not necessarily solved by the committed or procedural neutrality of the teacher and certainly do not imply that the subject must be excluded from a secular institution. Like the historian, the religious educator may reveal his (her) own commitment and must avoid any kind of indoctrination resulting from closed contents, methods, intentions and conclusions. In this way he will indicate to pupils the importance of commitment, whilst showing them how various religions and life-stances proceed and enabling them to engage in the search themselves.

Education in the Religious Dimension

So much then for those aspects and procedures of education which religious education shares with other subjects, and through which it shares their legitimacy. What, now, are the distinctive and particular aspects of religious education which may be clearly regarded as more than religious studies and which the religious educator (who may be a person of commitment but whose commitment does not necessarily prevent impartiality in educational procedure) will claim to be legitimate in secular institutions?

In the first place, in this aspect of the curriculum as nowhere else – unless the school has a distinct, coherent and comprehensive programme of personal and social education – the pupil will encounter fundamental issues of existence and consider the nature of personhood. For if education is concerned with the nature of persons – and with persons not in rational isolation but in community (their relationships and interaction, and their application of principles, personally and corporately, morally and socially) – then religious education has a great deal to contribute. It will educate pupils in the ways in which one or more religions deal with and enshrine all these aspects of personhood (though the skilful teacher with a shortage of time may, while concentrating on one religion, have to show pupils how to transfer from one viewpoint or situation to another). The skilful teacher will enable the pupils to use the skills of education to understand what it means to be a Christian or a Muslim in

this or that situation. Thus from a consideration of beliefs, or from existential situations, the pupils will proceed into an educated understanding;
and if this be regarded as too difficult, one may refer to the way in which
teachers repeatedly educate pupils into identifying with the Good Samaritan (though they may eschew the equally important task of understanding the attitudes of priest and Levite). Apart from the problem of religious
authority already mentioned at the end of the last section (page 88) (the
Bible, Qur'ān, Gita and natural theology being sometimes in conflict),
the teacher may have added difficulties in dealing with the application of
beliefs to practice, not merely because of the range of belief and practice in
any one religion (for example, on abortion, in Christianity), but also
because of variance in educational procedure (for example, the refusal of
Muslims to allow girls to be present at a teenage discussion on sexual relationships), but these and other difficulties do not undermine their
legitimacy.

At this stage it becomes clear that religious education is not only developing the cognitive understanding of religions and their differences but
also helping pupils in their attitudes, affections and practice to appreciate,
understand and live with diversity. In other words, the affective domain
of education is involved in the active development, in pupils, of sympathy, empathy, sensitivity and respect. A religious education which does
not develop these kinds of qualities may be regarded as being incomplete,
if not a failure. Of course, alongside this will go a critical evaluation of the
reasons for, and justifications of, such beliefs and practices; and the pupils
will learn that matters which are peripheral and secondary in one religion
are central and vital in another. So hand in hand with pupils' understanding of personhood, and their practice of self- and other-awareness, will go
their knowledge and use of the necessary skills, which are essential for the
truly religiously educated – rational discourse, critical evaluation, apologetics, an understanding of language and concepts (the status of sacred
writings and traditions, the basis of authority and the importance of history, events and persons, the place of the individual and of the community
experience, the way in which the absolute is communicated and its relationship to moral and social practice), and the practice of concern and
compassion and respect for others. And all this will be developed not
through impressionistic hearsay but within the framework and contents
of his acquired knowledge.

Secondly, the area of the spiritual, even though present in other (and
not merely aesthetic) subjects, is one which will be the special concern of
religious education. Although 'spiritual' is a term usually reserved for
theistic religions, the idea is present in Buddhism and the term is increasingly used by humanists, agnostics and even atheists to identify the non-
physical and non-rational realm of human experience and development.
For example, the scientist, confronted with the mystery of existence, and
the economist, aware of the inadequacy of materialistic motivation and
reward, join with the religious believer in stressing the importance of a
level of experience which transcends rationality and physical or material
satisfaction. At this point they are moving into the realm of personal and

interpersonal relationships and experience. Obviously there are in all religions and in the lives of holy people high moments of spiritual experience (even though the cynic may proffer a purely psychological explanation); equally there are particular activities, such as prayer and meditation, which are part of everyday religious life and designed to develop a person's spirituality. Both of these will be an obvious part of a knowledgeable understanding of religion, but the *practice* is so much part of the private mysteries of a religion that it should not form part of religious education in a secular institution (not even as a simulation exercise). Nevertheless there remain the depths of existence itself and the dynamic nature of man, which, in a world dominated by materialism and self-centredness, calls out not only for exploration but also development; and although the humanist would deny or doubt the spiritual eternity of personhood, many humanists would support a religious education which provoked spiritual insight and growth. The religious educator, of course, must enable the pupils to use a full range of cognitive and affective disciplines in order to distinguish the real from the spurious (a problem from within, as well as from outside, any religion); but he (she) will find allies for this task not only in art, music and literature but also, as we have seen, in mathematics and the sciences, where imagination and symbol and shape and orderliness may provoke enjoyment and wonder and so feed the human spirit. For example, that child may be partaking in spiritual development who has moved from the innocent wonder at creativity in pond-life through analytical studies in biology to an understanding that all existence is more than physical and involves a giving and a receiving. Moreover, this dimension is not only individual but corporate, for in this sense 'spiritual' deals with more than the principle of individuation. And such an education will undoubtedly open doors to the spiritual nature of existence in terms of an Absolute or of an evolutionary progression of life.

This leads to a third and distinctive contribution in religious education. It is difficult to categorise religions in one class, for their separate and exclusive claims to authority are compounded by the diversity of their approaches to the Absolute and to existence (even in Hinduism, that most inclusive of religions), and by the fact that the framework for study which satisfies one religion (and the framework most usually adopted is that of Christianity) is rarely properly acceptable to the insider of another religion. Once, however, the understanding of religion(s) is accepted as a field of educational activity, decisions about the legitimacy of its contents and procedures lie with the professional educators (and indirectly with the validating bodies); the only justifiable request from a religious group is that the educational activity does full justice to the true nature of that religion, with all its peculiar nuances. Nevertheless, this aspect of religious education, like the field of moral education where there are similar differences both about the ultimate and the procedural, provides one of the most creative educational activities. For the twentieth century has seen a growing dialogue between religions – and not merely in abstract theologising but as dialogue within community. All those values so important in personal development and in moral education – freedom and responsibility, honesty and compassion, reason and fairness, truth and respect, tolerance and commitment – are operating at a fundamental level when people talk to one another about the ultimate nature of existence and the way in which different religions understand the person in himself or herself and in his or her duties and relationships. And although teachers may have little scholastic claim to be part of that dialogue, they face its diversity in the classroom, so that truths and the perception of truths, in tension, are a legitimate, and perhaps major, contribution of religion to the education of pupils. It therefore becomes a vital part of the work of any school, secular or otherwise, that its pupils with their diverse backgrounds, and their future set in a diverse society and world, should be educated not only in understanding what motivates people at depth but also in reaching commitment themselves and in living with others of different commitments in a responsible and responsive manner. If secular society is to grow and if any consensus within it is to be achieved, then education has a vital part to play; religious education can make a unique contribution, therefore, not in studying abstract knowledge or fostering artificial consensus, but in the exploration of the similarities and differences in pattern and life-style offered by diverse religions. Whatever education may be offered at other times of the week for particular pupils by their faith communities, nevertheless, within a secular society, in County schools, the religious education described here must be provided by the same teacher at the same time in the same classroom for all pupils, for only in this way can it fully conform to the educational norms of such schools. It is against this background and within this context that pupils will be truly educated in religion and helped to formulate (without pressure) their own commitment and faith while recognising that such beliefs may not be final.

Conclusion

Religious education exists within education and must conform to the norms of educational activity, but it may also be legitimate for it to be seen as offering a challenge to it. It is not merely that its subject matter and, to some extent, its procedures are distinctive. It stands outside other subjects and forms of knowledge and asks questions, provoking insight like a Socratic gad-fly. It may be that it requires a particular approach to religious education to be committed and yet open, and it may be that not all religions are willing to encourage this approach, because they regard such openness as a denial of the ultimacy of their faith or as educationally dangerous (perhaps partly because they may never have experienced it). But it is one of the dangers of a secular institution that it may develop its own introvert autonomy; it is of the essence of both religion and education to challenge such introversion and to liberate the mind. Thus religious education is fundamental to the nature of education, whether as a body of knowledge, a realm of meaning, or as a process. As such it must be legitimate within any institution which is concerned with the whole person.

A Response to Howard W. Marratt

Ursula King

The Need to Foster Spirituality in Secular Institutions

When I was asked to respond to the paper of the Revd Howard Marratt, I was told to pay special attention to the question of how far secular institutions may be able to nurture spirituality. What follows had to be prepared independently, and thus is not a closely argued response but presents instead some complementary material, almost a series of footnotes rather than a step-by-step logical analysis of the preceding arguments. However, I wish to enlarge especially on one point made in the previous papers, the remark 'that the area of the spiritual. . .is one which will be the special concern of religious education'.[1]

I am not professionally closely involved in the debates surrounding religious education in schools but I work in the area of religious studies and have a special interest in questions of spirituality and mysticism in world religions. During this Consultation such questions as what may be the common and diverging interests of religious education in general and the nurture into a specific faith will be raised. These issues are closely related to the current debates surrounding the study of religion, especially within a multicultural society where the different world faiths now meet within the confines of every city, if not every classroom. I am acquainted with the empirical and logical reasons for a multifaith religious education and am aware of the sophisticated analytical tools used in the debate about religious education. But these tools are also incredibly theoretical and abstract and I do not know how far they may not simply be, to quote a criticism levelled at other academic disciplines, the parading of habitual professional skills displayed largely for the admiration of one's peers. Like so much else, the debate about religious education seems to suffer from the main cancer of Western culture and education in general: it is over-rationalistic with a high development of the critical faculties of discernment at the expense of emotional and experiential modes of being, with the result that it does not sufficiently form the heart and emotions of our young.

It is sometimes easier for a non-specialist to speak more directly, with less intellectual sophistication perhaps but with more experience and power of vision, and thus go straight to the heart of the matter. I shall later quote such a more direct approach to questions of spirituality which I have found particularly illuminating.

For the moment I want to ask a very specific question: can avowedly secular institutions promote studies which may intend to or can in fact nurture spirituality? In other words, can religious education be taught in a manner which provides more than a secular analysis of religion, an education which helps to develop interiority, a spirit of worship, gratitude and adoration, respect, love and compassion for the otherness of one's neighbours, and also the will to build up closer ties of community in peace and justice? You will notice that my understanding of spirituality is not merely an interior, contemplative one relating to the dispositions of the individual; on the contrary, it is closely tied up with the shaping of the outside world and with active values. As the former United Nations Secretary-General and mystic Dag Hammarskjöld has said, 'In our age the road to holiness [I might add, to 'spirituality'] passes through action.'

Much progress has been made in Britain in the teaching of religious education in a spirit of openness; there is a genuine fostering of understanding of the values enshrined in different world religions. This is a great step forward, especially in educating the young and ourselves in living in a world of religious and cultural pluralism. There is still considerable room for improvement here, however, for so much remains to be done, not only in schools but in the training of teachers and especially of theologians and ministers.

I should like to quote here the information gathered by the Birmingham group AFFOR (All Faith for One Race) in their report *Blind Leaders for the Blind?*, which was based on a survey of several colleges training people of different denominations for the ministry. This survey showed the ignorance of those trained for the ministry of the knowledge and skills which would enable them to deal with the current multifaith situation in Britain. One of the questions asked was, 'Would you say that the teaching of New Testament and Old Testament studies, ethics and doctrine, is given within a world context?' The majority replied to this question with 'No.' 72% of the respondents said they had not been prepared by their college courses for the multifaith situation in Britain, whereas over 90% agreed that it was necessary to teach world religions in schools. This report has much other valuable information and gives food for thought to those involved in teaching theology and religious studies in our various educational institutions whether religious or secular.[2] It not only reveals the relative lack of knowledge about world religions in the training of one particular group of people, but it also emphasises the need for teaching in a *global context*, a point of the greatest importance to which I shall return shortly.

It is important to distinguish that the necessary knowledge about more faiths than one's own, the knowledge *about* world religions and cultures, is the absolutely essential basis to begin with, but that this knowledge by itself does not necessarily provide a religious education as others have argued in detail, nor the necessary education in spirituality which seems to me an indispensable requirement for learning to give meaning to one's life.

Many religious education teachers use Ninian Smart's analysis of the phenomena of religion into six dimensions. It is very illuminating indeed to *look at* the social, ritual, experiential, doctrinal, mythic and ethical dimensions in different religions, but where is the spiritual dimension here? Is it part of the experiental, the mythic, the ethical, or is it implicit in any of the other dimensions? Is part of the reason for the absence of the spiritual dimension here perhaps the fact that we still *look at* religion from outside rather than try with empathy to get truly inside it, close to its centre and core? Whilst it is absolutely necessary to disseminate information and knowledge *about* world religions at every level of our educational institutions, the decisive issue is surely *what meaning* we assign to this knowledge. How do we interpret, apply and use it at a practical level? It is here that it can be argued that spiritual education, or education towards spiritual values and spirituality, is an important and necessary ingredient, just as moral education is; in fact, the two are in many ways closely intertwined.

Some may immediately object that education for spirituality is part of religious nurture and therefore does not belong in the secular school. I would argue differently, that we need to approach, understand and practise spirituality in a pluralistic perspective rather than simply from the point of view of nurture into one specific faith, and that the discovery of the spiritual dimension in human beings should be part of the whole educational process of *educare*, of drawing out and actualising human potential to the full. We have to look at what unites rather than what divides the different religious faiths, and the distinctiveness of the different religious traditions can now only be meaningfully understood in the light of *togetherness*. A pluralistic perspective today must of necessity also be a convergent one, otherwise pluralism will create further divisions, discord and tension – a fragmentation which will not help us to shape a better world of greater peace and justice.

Readers may or may not be aware that Teilhard de Chardin (1881–1955), whose birth centenary was celebrated only recently, was one of the early observers of our planet Earth who emphasised again and again the need to give full attention to the phenomenon of spirituality in our approach to religion – that is to say, to look at spirituality from a universal, global point of view. In fact, as early as 1937 he wrote an essay especially devoted to 'The Phenomenon of Spirituality' wherein he pleaded that we need technicians and engineers of the spiritual energies of the world to awaken and develop the sense of one world, of one human family. If we do not pay attention to nourishing the life of the spirit within us, we shall lose the zest and love for life, the will to work for a better quality of life, for building up one world together in a spirit of love and unification rather than hatred and division. Teilhard was emphatic in saying that it is necessary for the religions to change in order to meet the new needs of our world today, and it is equally necessary to develop a new morality and ethics. In fact, he saw the value of human action as defined by three principles:

1 *only* finally good is what makes for the growth of the spirit on earth;
2 good (at least basically and partially) is *everything* that brings spiritual growth to the world;
3 finally, *best* is what assures the highest development to the spiritual powers of the earth.[3]

I cannot deal with Teilhard de Chardin's understanding of spirituality in detail here,[4] but would just like to mention that the phenomenon of spirituality plays a central role in his thought about the development of humanity from the past into the present and future. The spiritualities lived and taught by sages, saints and mystics through the ages form an inalienable and irreplaceable element of the global religious heritage of humankind. He considered this experience of spirituality as a linking and unifying feature of the different world religions which now, in a more and more interdependent world, interact upon each other, drawing together towards what he called 'a new mysticism' where spiritual principles, most of all those of love, need to animate and permeate our life of action. Teilhard saw the growth of consciousness and the growth of spirit as closely interlinked so that the growth of reason and the growth of love, of the loving forces of the heart, are not seen in opposition to each other but as interdependent.

In an age which is often considered as spiritually impoverished the themes of spirituality and mysticism have nevertheless come much more to the fore of attention since Teilhard de Chardin's days. This is evident not only from the number of publications in this field, but from the many efforts to 'explore inner space',[5] or the pursuit of an inner ecology which complements the search for an outer ecological balance in the world. We now hear it even from the highest political quarters that spirituality should be a more central concern of our lives. This, at least, is the persuasively argued view of Robert Muller, the current Assistant Secretary-General of the United Nations, who in 1982 published a very inspiring book on this subject entitled *New Genesis: Shaping a global spirituality*.[6]

I should like to enlarge on Muller's views as they have considerable bearing on our topic of developing spirituality within a secular educational context and fit most appropriately into the overall international framework of this Consultation. Muller follows closely the thinking of the former United Nations Secretary-General U Thant who attached the greatest importance to spirituality (U Thant in turn was

influenced by both the thinking of Albert Schweitzer and that of Teilhard
de Chardin). U Thant saw the needs of the individual and of humanity as a
whole in terms of four different stages, the physical, mental, moral and
spiritual. Muller has described these stages in 'The Four Cries of
Humanity' as the cry for physical development, the cry for mental fulfilment, the cry for morality and the cry for spirituality. Whilst the United
Nations is doing much for the physical and mental well-being of humanity
and is perhaps also fostering a new world morality, it has not yet given
room to spirituality in its work. Muller sees this as the next and necessary
step in the further evolution of the global work of the United Nations.

Although a traditional Roman Catholic by background, Muller did not
discover either the need for or the wealth of the world's spiritualities until
he had worked at the United Nations for many years. This great experience in practical internationalism lived in a multicultural, secular context
has made him see not only the need for an altogether new type of education in our secular educational institutions, namely the need for a global
educational framework, but it has also made him experience the need for a
global approach to religion and spirituality.

Looking at the globe and its humanity as one, Muller says that there are
about 5000 religions on this planet, not all of whch can be studied and
evaluated by every individual. Individuals are usually born into a religion
– or one might add, they are born into a completely secular life without
any religion, at least in many of our Western urban centres – but they
must learn through education to open up and grow outwards from their
own limited background and experience so that they come to realise that
our modern world is not only shaped by more and more material interdependencies but also by the interdependencies of our mental and spiritual
lives.

Muller is just as aware as other discerning minds that the development
of interiority and spirituality is conspicuously lagging behind our enor-
mously impressive advances in science and technology, and yet he can still
say that the development of science itself can be seen as part of a spiritual
process at work within humankind, though we must now unite the practice of science with that of love!

What we need today is a sense of direction, an education for further
progress in interiority (the dimension concerned with the self), in morality (concerned with the self, others and the world) and in spirituality (concerned with the dimension of transcendence) to bring about the unification of the world rather than its disintegration. The contemporary world
is marked by the profound paradox that on one hand it is deeply torn and
divided through many groups enhancing their own identity and separate-
ness at the expenses of others, whilst on the other hand there are very
powerful movements of unification, of peace and liberation, of experiments in new community-living, based on the bonds of human sisterhood
and brotherhood.

Many voices say today that humanity is ready for a new culture, for a
new age. This 'new age' thinking is particularly powerful among the
young, but it is found across all ages, all races, all cultures and both sexes.

Muller observes 'that it is difficult to hold together any human group for long if there is not a vision, an ideal, an objective, a dream. To bind the human family together, to foster its further ascent, to prevent it from losing ground and falling into an abyss of despair, we must have a constant vision, a dream for the human family.'[7] Although the dreams of peace, world fraternity and the United Nations are often scoffed at, we need to have faith in them to make them come true. For Muller the key to the future is education, global education and spiritual education, so that we can learn to live together *in spite of* and *with* our diversities. In this context of a necessary world ecumenism and convergence Muller assigns a specially important role to religions. He feels that the religions have many of the answers which the political world is seeking – they have given us 'generally correct codes of conduct, codes of internal serenity, codes of happiness, codes for the highest fulfilment of the miracle of life'.[8] But today, with an acceleration of social and political changes, the world's major religions must speed up dramatically their ecumenical movement and recognise the unity of their objectives in the diversity of their cults.[9] In other words, they must not consider their own religious rites and traditions as more valuable than universal spirituality. If they do, it only increases tension in the world and does not foster cooperation.

It is Muller's dream to provide such a forum for the cooperation of religions which may help to shape a global spirituality at the United Nations. In fact, he mentions that many at the United Nations consider the secular achievement of the cooperation among all nations practised at the United Nations as a kind of new religion, a supreme path or way. Muller is firmly convinced that spiritual education towards a universal, global spirituality will make a world of difference: it will create an altogether different world. And this perspective has grown out of the experience of the world's largest secular institution!

The sceptic will reply, 'This is too vague, too indefinite and so universal as to be non-specific.' All spiritualities, as all mysticisms, deal with particular paths, particular ways, particular *sadhanas*, to use an Hindu term. This is in fact the crux of the matter: how to learn to relate and creatively integrate the particular with the universal, or to use a phrase from the previous contribution, 'how to be committed yet remain open'. By the particular I mean our own limited background, our particular faith or doctrinal commitment, or the fact that some of our contemporaries have no religious conviction at all. To integrate this with a growing openness to the different and sometimes difficult and contradictory beliefs of others so that we grow outwards and can embrace other visions which enlarge or, as the case may be, contradict or complement our own. Here I think of the example of Gandhi who spoke of opening the windows of his own house to the winds from the outside world without being swept off his feet. Every individual needs to be deeply rooted in his or her own tradition but also has to learn to grow upwards and outwards like the many branches of a large tree. It is important to remember here that the study of religion and the increasing knowledge we have gathered about religious phenomena around the world may also have an effect *on changing religious awareness.* Today we speak of trans-national cooperations and we have many trans-national new religious movements, especially among the young; there are also many who work for a new trans-disciplinary approach to knowledge in order to overcome outdated and rigidly ossified boundaries of traditional disciplines. Similarly, we might look for a kind of trans-national and trans-religious 'world-believer', for someone who has a fuller religious consciousness which transcends the traditionally divisive religious boundaries and integrates various elements from different religious traditions. Furthermore, it is important not only to perceive the changing role of religion and the greater emphasis on spirituality within the world today but also to discern the new developments in the relationship between religion and science, particularly as expressed among certain nuclear physicists and radio astronomers who see a close affinity between our present understanding of energy, matter and the nature of the cosmos, and the perennial insights of religious people, particularly of the mystics.

To look further ahead, will the current revolution in electronics, in the development of communications and information technology, profoundly affect and alter our practice, understanding and teaching of religion? It certainly will have an impact which we cannot ignore, although developments in this field may be difficult to assess at present. We should prepare ourselves in our educational institutions to develop new educational strategies to educate the next generations for tomorrow's rather than yesterday's world. Our world is a thoroughly secular world, but, for those who can see it, there is a spiritual dimension within secularity itself. From a religious perspective all life and work is sacred and the whole world can be seen as a cosmic sacrament. I would like to mention here the important distinction between secularity, secularisation and secularism. Secularity refers to the intrinsic value and autonomy of our world and work, whereas secularisation is the process by which this autonomy is being achieved. This is a process of transformation and change which can be positively understood as a process of growth, whilst secularism may be understood negatively as a process of stunted growth whereby secular values come to be seen as an end in themselves with no more openness to the transcendent.

For many, modern secular consciousness is undergoing a profound mutation which expresses itself also in the transformation of religious awareness, in the search for a new holistic spirituality which is world-transforming rather than world-fleeing and which can discern many signs of revelation in contemporary secular culture, in the fields of politics and education, in the idealism of the young, in the quests of contemporary feminism, in the spiritual thirst and hunger for liberation expressed in ever so many different movements today. Can one nurture spirituality in secular institutions of education? What is the answer to this question? Is it or is it not possible? Does it or does it not happen?

As I see it at present, my answer is that very often it does not happen, but it does not happen much in theological or religious institutions either. Speaking from my own educational experience in theological institutions in Germany, France and Britain, I can hardly think of any more 'demy-thologising' and 'secularising' process than modern over-rationalistic theological studies which give no or, at the most, very little room to spirit-uality. Spirituality has long been divorced from theology and, conse-quently, spiritual life has been orphaned. It has remained underdeveloped, so that more and more people begin to recognise the spiritual impoverish-ment of our generation.

Spiritual education can give a sense of direction to a world more and more marked by the need for an orientation towards understanding our basic choices. Such education can mediate insight and meaning and present life-enhancing values. But can such spiritual education be under-taken in the secular school? Mr Marratt said that we must convey an understanding of spirituality but 'practice cannot be part of the school'.[10] I am not so sure about this. It really depends on what is meant by practice. Is it a divisive rite or an exercise in interiority, in meditation, in the search of the spiritual in us? By way of example I would like to mention the article 'Can we do that candle thing again?' by Lynne Scholefield,[11] and two excellent books which pupils in the Sixth Form would certainly find very stimulating, Martin Israel's fine study *Summons to Life: The Search for Identity through the Spiritual*,[12] or the more recent work by Donald Nicholl on *Holiness*.[13] Both works, though predominantly Christian, draw on material from different world religions. There is also the splendid new resource given to us by the publication (by Paulist Press) of the series 'Classics of Western Spirituality', soon to be complemented by 'Classics of Eastern Spirituality'. Fordham University in New York already offers under Professor Ewert Cousins a 'Spirituality Programme' for university students, and undoubtedly pupils in the upper forms at school would greatly benefit from a similar course of studies. Robert Muller's book, which I quoted earlier, would make an excellent start for such a develop-ment of education towards spirituality.

So far the stages of moral development in the individual have been charted with great sophistication, and the insights of these researches have been incorporated into moral and religious education in schools and colleges. However, the stages of the spiritual development and growth of the individual, although much commented upon by spiritual writers and mystics, have not yet been given sufficient attention in contemporary educational theories. One might almost say that their comprehensive secular analysis is now urgently required.

Secular institutions can and must develop education for spiritual values if the world is to survive. They can nurture spirituality in a global, pluralistic perspective with a genuine openness towards the religious and spiritual quest of our contemporaries in a way in which traditional reli-gious institutions often cannot because they are too much bound up with and tied to the particularities of their own religious tradition. Secular educational institutions can and must help to shape a global spirituality. If they can envisage this aim and work towards it, they will create, in the words of Robert Muller's book, a truly 'New Genesis' by bringing into birth and life the vision of a new world.

Notes and References

1 See MARRATT, H. W., 'The Legitimacy of Religious Education in Secular Institutions', page 89 in this volume.
2 This report is available from AFFOR, 173 Lozells Road, Lozells, Birmingham, B19 1HS.
3 See TEILHARD DE CHARDIN, P., 'The phenomenon of spirituality', in his book *Human Energy* (trans. 1969). London: Collins (93–112).
4 For a longer discussion, see KING, U. (1980) *Towards a New Mysticism. Teilhard de Chardin and Eastern Religions.* London: Collins.
5 See HAY, D. (1982) *Exploring Inner Space.* London: Penguin.
6 (1982) New York: Doubleday.
7 MULLER, R., op. cit., page 19.
8 Ibid., page 43.
9 Ibid., page 183.
10 MARRATT, H. W., op. cit., page 90 in this volume
11 In *British Journal of Religious Education*, Spring 1983 (84–6).
12 (1974; reprinted 1979) London: Hodder and Stoughton.
13 (1981) London: Darton, Longman and Todd.

Religious Education – Truth-claims or Meaning-giving?

Daniel W. Hardy

You will quickly see from this title that facing it adequately will place us in the midst of all the most basic problems about religious education. And not only those of religious education: the problems are also those of theology, philosophy, and education *per se* – areas which we must traverse together in order to find a satisfactory answer to the question set in the title. We shall attempt to face these problems directly initially, with minimal reference to religious education, and then explore their implications for religious education.

Concern about meaning seems to be central to present-day religious education, which is often claimed to have as its purpose to 'stimulate within the pupils, and assist them in the search for, a personal sense of meaning in life'.[1] But what such a 'sense of meaning in life' is, is somewhat less clear, and not often elucidated. And at first sight, it seems a concern which is alien to directly religious concerns.

The genesis of this preoccupation with meaning is in the modern idealists' investigations of the conditions and structures of 'consciousness', which had direct antecedents in Aquinas' understanding of the illuminative power of human mind and Luther's concern with subjectivity. Kant had analyzed the regulative laws which operated in cognition and morality, but others 'completed' his programme by adding the content which his way had (by its own admission) lacked, through tracing the universal history and phenomenology of consciousness. This, they thought, would show the way by which human consciousness appropriated itself through its relationship with itself, the world and God. Such a programme is seen in Hegel, for example. But that speculative attempt required correction, especially with the distresses produced by the transformations of civilisation in the industrial revolution, and that correction came through the influence of the natural sciences, which served as a model. In place of a speculatively formulated phenomenology of consciousness, imposed on history, there came a new emphasis on actual experience. It is experience which provides the data of meaning in which can be found both the action of consciousness and the *what* (whether pertaining to the world or to God) to be interpreted.

What this new emphasis on experience does is to make experience, seen in *units*, what is *given*. But these units of experience are also units of *meaning*, whose significance has been grasped through the activity of consciousness, or through the intending of the 'I' who experiences. So, while there is new emphasis on experience here, there is also insistence on the activity of consciousness in apprehending meaning – neither simply receiving experience passively nor simply transferring its own innate ideas and structures on to experience, but actively establishing meaning in experience. What is more, this activity can both extend the experiencing subject and offer an enlarged medium for establishing the meaning of what is experienced. I say 'can' because it does not *necessarily* do so: whether it does so, and illuminates subject and what is experienced, depends on *how* the activity is done – whether the activity of consciousness offers 'space' for the experienced to be what it is, while at the same time extending itself to be capable of appreciating the full meaning of what is experienced.

An example will help us to understand. Suppose the treasurer of an organisation is faced with the task of putting the financial affairs of the organisation in order and satisfying the public that the organisation's finances are sound. What is important in this task is units of information or experience which are already assigned meaning as 'income' or 'expenditure' simply by virtue of being payments received or payments made, and they are so recorded in the books. Beyond this point, accepted accountancy conventions become involved, and the treasurer must *extend* his 'living' to include living with these units of experience with the meaning established for them by these conventions, until the organisation's finances can be mapped fully through the structures provided by those conventions. For one who does not do such things all the time, doing this job can be a struggle: he must acquire (live) the semiotics of an accountant and utilize them to such a point that he can be productive in establishing the meaning of the finances of the organisation – that is, allow the figures to be what they are and also appreciate their full meaning (for example, whether the books balance and whether there is a sufficient balance in hand to allow the organisation to continue). The whole process requires the extension of the treasurer and of the medium for establishing the meaning of what he (she) experiences: he must be extended in order to establish the meaning more fully. Furthermore, the basis for this is his commitment to the task, his responsibility, and his capacity and freedom to be extended. In the absence of an ongoing commitment of life, it is remarkable how quickly his acquired capacities diminish to the point of being vestigial – and how quickly he becomes a financial machine.

But still more is involved where wider issues than these are at stake. Even in a limited situation such as the treasurer's just mentioned, there are important matters of meaning at issue, where the treasurer must in effect *refind* himself in order to establish the meaning of his experience more fully. There must be a matching between a new self-appropriation and a new establishment of the meaning of experience; and he cannot acknowledge himself as treasurer until that is achieved, nor can others recognise him as such until it is clear that this has occurred – until they recognise his establishment of the meaning of his experience as a presentation of the meaning of the organisation's life. He has 'done it for them' in a sense, but his work must be accepted by an 'academic' (the accountant) and by 'society' (in this case, the membership of the organisation).[2] In either case, it is not simply an acceptance of its 'factuality' which these members make, but a review of its meaning as the meaning of the organisation's life, which requires that they extend themselves in order to establish whether the treasurer's 'meaning' is a 'meaning' which they are prepared to see for the organisation.

Though we are already deep in issues which are important for modern understanding and for religious education, we have so far only discussed meaning in the case of a particular instance of meaning where provisional meaning is all that is required. That is not to be treated lightly, because even in such a case the meaning which is established serves as the basis for further life. For the treasurer to find, and others to accept, the meaning of the organisation's life, is to provide a way forward for that life. Indeed, what the treasurer is doing is to find the meaning of the organisation's life at a particular time *in order to* ascertain the way forward. In other words, his work is part of a process by which the wider meaning of the organisation – its goal – is established at the moment, and its continuance anticipated.

Implicit in these activities – in the extension of the treasurer's understanding, in the fuller establishment of the meaning of his experience of the organisation, in his self-appropriation and that of the members of the organisation, in the establishment and anticipation of its wider meaning (or goal) – is reference to higher and wider notions of meaning, and beyond them to a notion of meaning which has its meaning in itself absolutely, without the need for reference to anything else. Hence all understanding of meaning is enclosed in an all-embracing meaning:

> The knowledge of partial truths, of individual spheres of creation and of the history of the world and mankind, as well as the investigation of the material world in its usefulness for man, in short, whatever wants to share in the act of understanding, it all remains enclosed in the all-embracing form of it which gives all knowledge its meaning.[3]

So any establishment of meaning, with the correlative extension of the finder of meaning and his (her) new self-appropriation, both in the process of anticipating the future, requires justification in the perspective of the whole.

Actually, this is sometimes claimed, both in theory and practice, to be an 'optional extra' in establishment of meaning. Those who are concerned with the brain as a neural network of interacting neurons (like a bowlful of alphabet soup) insist that meaning is an optional feature which may emerge as a consequence of evolutionary environmental pressures (just as one may construct sentences from the letters in the soup). If such is one's conviction, there is no reason to suppose an all-embracing meaning; but even on this view one can argue for a universal meaning. Others avoid the possibility of an all-embracing meaning by pragmatic means, by declaring it sufficient to establish the meaning of something in itself – by reference only to the area of concern at the moment, and without wider considerations.

Whether such counterclaims are acceptable depends very much on how this all-embracing meaning impinges on our establishment of meaning in a particular instance. Remembering that self-extension and self-appropriation through finding the meaning of experience, and doing so in anticipation of a wider meaning or goal, were essential characteristics of meaning-finding, what we would expect of an all-embracing meaning is that it would enter into such activities to provide them with the *possibility of fulfilment*. We would also expect that it would enable us to *justify* what we were doing, and confirm the process by which we are finding meaning. In other words, I should be enabled by it to 'find myself in agreement with myself in such a way that it is in agreement with my world'.[4] That may happen in a moment, but such a moment will properly prefigure and lead to an agreement with my being as a whole which is also an agreement with beings as whole – to a full self-appropriation through responsibility to others in the world. The proportioning of my self and my relation to the world (and others whom I experience) takes place through the all-embracing meaning; and I am free to find the meaning in the world (and others), and therefore in myself, by being open and responsible to that all-embracing meaning – or, if 'the core of all meaning is being' (Lonergan),[5] by being open and responsible to that being.

The presence or accessibility of such an all-embracing meaning is by no means unquestioned, whether because of the apparent meaninglessness of occurrences in life (in suffering, pain, for example), or of life itself (in the face of boredom and death, or of self-loathing). And it is subject to vastly different constructions, amongst which are to be found many which are intrinsically self-limiting – unable to provide a possibility of fulfilment of the kind already mentioned, because they are extra-worldly, anti-individual, collectivist, vacuous and so on. There are many tricky issues involved in sorting out which versions of this all-embracing meaning actually suffice. This task need not occupy us here, except to recognise that a tacit agreement about what an all-embracing meaning does and should do in providing fulfilment in the ordinary activities of meaning-establishment will determine what are acceptable versions of it. That is, the very process of meaning-establishment will show what notion of an all-embracing meaning may be present in that process. That will be the criterion for including some notions as properly 'religious' and excluding others, for establishing the selection of what counts as 'religious' in religious education.

To say this is not to suggest that there is anything 'necessary' in the presence of this all-embracing meaning, that it is so unambiguously present as to render anyone who disputes it a self-blinding fool. It can be suggested that the whole process of finding oneself (self-appropriation) through establishing the meaning of experience, made possible by an all-embracing meaning, is based on the notion of an external and immutable *logos* permeating everything and enabling a person to find himself or herself in finding meaning. Thus it relocates in the human consciousness what has been the action of the divine Word in the world. And this notion, so the claim goes, must be 'deconstructed'. Instead, we must see that meanings are generated quite differently, 'not by addition, but by differentiation, dislocation, or distortion'.[6] Hence, meaning does not arise by the addition of meaning to experience referred to, but by the creative use of language which occurs as old meanings are 'bent' to create new, and meaning becomes 'pure movement, the overflowing self-effacement of language'[7] – a movement which reveals all substance, all that is outside the movement of meaning, as emptiness. Likewise, one cannot search for Being or Truth; that is the ultimate projection of grammar.

Following the line of this 'deconstruction', we see how fragile is the possibility afforded by an all-embracing meaning to the process of self-appropriation through meaning. We can readily see how some dispute the presence of an all-embracing meaning, and disallow the importance of religious education (for example) as a 'fumbling after shadows'. In fact, the very fragility of the presence of this all-embracing meaning presents an important challenge, for what defence can religious educators offer for the notion which is central to their subject? Indeed, what defence can theologians offer? It seems to me that the defence for *religious educators* lies precisely in providing for the establishment of meaning which gives the possibility for self-appropriation which shows the presence of an all-embracing meaning, and for *theologians* in recognising the consequences of such a thing for the nature of the all-embracing meaning. In other words, religious educators can work *expansively* with meaning and self-appropriation, lifting particular experiences into a more complex pattern of meaning or a wider horizon, and thereby find the presence of the all-embracing meaning which had been present in earlier religious meaning: they can recollect the earlier presence by finding it anew. Theologians can understand that the all-embracing meaning is not only found, nor is it determinatively formed, in the past; it is formed in the generative power present in expanding meaning. There has already been considerable progress, amongst theologians anyway, along these lines.

Implicit throughout our discussion so far has been the issue of truth, and we must now turn directly to it, difficult though it is. Even in the relatively simple case of the treasurer, he is expected to be truthful in assigning meaning and appreciating the fuller meaning of the organisation's financial position – truthful in his experience, truthful in finding meaning, truthful in assessing the wider meaning or goal of the organisation, and truthful to himself, to the organisation, and truthful by reference to the all-embracing meaning of things.

Through much of history, truth was supposed to be an external court of appeal, the Being or Will or Word of God; and that divine Truth was to remain the goal of all human knowledge and effort, even if itself known only in a limited way through faith or knowledge. But, parallel to the new concern for the meaning of experience which we discussed earlier, truth was reformulated: now it was no longer agreement with God's truth but 'agreement with the laws of the intellect' or the achievement of all that is necessary for the synthetic unity of experience (Kant). So truth is no longer external to experience and meaning, but that for which experience and meaning strive and which *comes to be* in thought and practice. And it is extremely important as an ideal.

A further step is made when we ask, with Nietzsche, what truth *means* as a concept. What is it that is sought by this ideal, truth? Is it simply a matter of being a truthful man in a truthful world, in order to preclude falseness and deception, so that we can (in the terms of our earlier discussion) achieve full self-appropriation in the meaning we find in others and in the world? That, attractive as it is, is an ascetic path which makes us want other selves and another world, and search for them and that which makes them possible, by creating another world of (ideal) meaning – a superior, complete life in contrast to the life that we have. This can be done in various ways – for example, by the elevation of a certain kind of morality, or a special form of knowledge, or a religious realm. These ways are then coercively imposed as norms by which ordinary life, knowledge, and world are to be corrected.

Much of the impetus of present British life has been gained by means of such ideals: Christianity has largely been replaced by moralism, which continues some of its interests by other means; and 'knowledge is the continuation of morality and religion but by other means'.[8] And such ideals deeply permeate the educational environment, vying with each other in importance. Interestingly, the desirability of knowledge goes largely unquestioned amongst educators, and so also does a certain code of morality which is socialised in British society. But more stringent and over-arching ideals of behaviour are seen as moral *claims* suggested by some people, as though they were a kind of 'party politics'; likewise, a religious 'world' of meaning, in which ideal knowledge and morality are presented, is marginalised as the special *claim* or interest of those who are religious, and still further muted by being considered, even by religious educators, as comprised of various truth-*claims*. In other words, there is a distinct 'pecking order' amongst ideals: knowledge and societally-accepted moral codes are 'true' and do not require special pleading; more 'ideal' kinds of knowledge and morality are truth-*claims* and do require special apology.

Part of the explanation for this state of affairs is the way in which the 'ascetic path' has been pursued. The legitimate task of meaning – achieving full self-appropriation in the meaning we find in others and in the word – has been pursued by creating *another world* of ideal meaning, deemed to be true and thus distinct from the falseness of the natural world. This has been perpetuated by those with an 'interest' in it, and who to some extent 'live' it, while at the same time others (and even they themselves) inhabit a different world and appropriate themselves through the meaning they find in that. So there has arisen a split between that detached and ideal truth, on the one hand, and this natural world of meaning: the two are in uneasy mutual confrontation, two kinds of meaning and experience.

But the other part of the explanation for this state of affairs is the way in which 'normalcy' has been pursued. The task of meaning has been severely reduced, by tacit agreement; and the ideal of truth has been left vacuous and undetermined, incapable of challenging anyone and lending force to the problem of self-appropriation in the meaning found in others and the world. Thus knowledge, morality and (where treated) religion are domesticated and, under the disguise of making them 'understandable', deprived of their ideal character – made 'safe'. They are the artifacts of a base, heavy and leaden soul. Where this is so, it is no wonder that the excitement and motivating power of a higher ideal of truth is sought elsewhere, either in the 'other world' of ideal meaning created and maintained through the pursuit of the 'ascetic path', or in some other ideal world privately or socially constructed. But such attempts to recapture the ideal only produce once again the split between 'normalcy' and the detached ideal. So we are left with the disjunction of a normalcy established by social or educational conventions from the ideal meaning-worlds perpetuated by religious people, each somewhat disconcerted by the other.

The problem – that from the viewpoint of 'normalcy' all such ideals as are fostered by religious people are 'claims', and that from the viewpoint of religious people 'normal' means of self-appropriation through establishing meaning are problematic because so far from ideal – is considerably exacerbated by the plurality of what is 'normal' and of what is 'ideal'. That is, the problem of truth is magnified 'at both ends': it is as difficult to establish unified desiderata for knowledge and morality as it is to establish what is common to the ideal meaning-worlds presented by (for example) religious people. That is why one can only use singular notions as 'knowledge' or 'religion' with the greatest caution, and why attempts to do so end by either dwelling on surface (non-ideal) characteristics (for example, Hick's analysis of knowledge as experiencing-as, or Smart's phenomenology of religious experience)[9] or losing the specificity of religious ideals in a phenomenology of ideals, as does Frithjof Schuon:

> All religion and all wisdom is reducible, extrinsically and from the human standpoint, to these four laws: enshrined in every tradition is to be observed an Immutable Truth, then a law of 'attachment to the Real', of 'remembrance' or 'love' of God, and finally prohibitions and injunctions; and these make up a fabric of elementary certainties which encompasses and resolves human uncertainty, and thus reduces the whole problem of earthly existence to a geometry that is at once simple and primordial.[10]

So there is a double need in the consideration of truth: how to find a unity between the 'normal' means of self-appropriation through establishing meaning and the 'ideal' means of doing so presented by religious people, and how to find a unity between the desiderata of the ideal meaning-worlds of various religious positions. These are important *critical* tasks for education as a whole and religious educators, as well as for religious people and theologians. And in general, the task should serve to expose all baseness of thought, and the various mystifications which abound in the consideration of such issues.

Our concern has been with self-appropriation through establishing meaning in experience of others and the world, seen earlier to be made possible through the presence of an all-embracing meaning. Likewise, now that we have considered the meaning of truth, we have seen that it is the ideal which draws us to do this in the fullest way, achieving full self-appropriation through fully responsible establishment of meaning, but without losing touch with ordinary experience and without losing touch with the deepest and most specific characteristics of the ideals fostered by the meaning-worlds of religious people. Truth, in other words, is the highest unity of meaning, and of self-appropriation through the establishment of meaning.

Such a unity cannot already have been fully achieved, because 'unity of truth can now only be thought of as the history of truth, meaning in effect that truth itself has a history and that its essence is the process of this history' (Pannenberg).[11] In other words, the unity of truth is finally achieved only at the end, and all prior self-appropriations through the establishment of meanings look forward to that; it 'completes' them, as they 'anticipate' it. Of course, this applies also to the self-appropriation through establishment of meaning which took place in distant places and times. The very process of history can single out some such 'acts of meaning' as crucially important, perhaps even essential to the unity of truth – as would be the case with certain contributions to knowledge. Still more important, history can single out some acts of self-appropriation through the establishment of meaning for others and the world which are of determinative importance as presenting the ideal in ordinary experience; and these can be brought forward – lifted into a more complex pattern of meaning or a wider horizon – as determinative anticipations of the final unity of truth.

So we have to look forward to, and work for, a unity between 'normal' or 'ordinary' ways of self-appropriation through meaning-giving, and the 'ideal' ways of doing so maintained by religious people; but we have also to work for, and look forward to, unity amongst the 'normal' ways and amongst the 'ideal' ways. And we now see that unity in such meanings is an historical process anticipating a completion in a highest unity of truth which has yet to be achieved.

We do not proceed with these tasks empty-handed, of course. Far from it: if anything, we are continually overwhelmed by the number of aids to meaning-giving which are available. Selection, and proper criteria for selection, are very important. For we are guided by some and we must see who they are – from Newton and Einstein to Darwin to the great religious figures whose 'acts of meaning' are of central importance. Their contributions are varied, some (despite their prominence in certain quarters) far more limited than others: work like Newton's or Einstein's is undoubtedly far-reaching in its significance, but it does not reach to the depth of personal self-appropriation through the giving of meaning which is achieved by (say) Muhammad or Jesus; and hence is not of such universal significance. Such 'acts of meaning', particularly those with a depth of personal self-appropriation, can be of determinative significance as presenting the ideal in ordinary experience. But that significance is only realised where they are, again and again, brought forward through fresh self-appropriations in meaning-giving in wider horizons. In other words, where those acts of meaning are expanded in new situations, their meaning can become a more nearly universal meaning, advance determinations of the final unity of truth. After all, the importance of Newton, Einstein and Darwin is in their extension and adaptation to new experience; likewise, the authority of Muhammad and Jesus emerges as and when their self-appropriation in meaning-giving becomes the form by which we appropriate ourselves in meaning-giving in quite different situations. Such truth can only be found in use; and even in use it seems inexhaustible, an unlimited anticipation of the final unity of truth. But how the truth of Einstein and Darwin and the great religious figures will finally be seen in the unity of truth remains to be seen.

From this, it is plain that these major figures are not simply prime 'examples' of what might be called 'competence' in meaning-giving. To see them as such is to place far too great a division between self-appropriation in meaning-giving and that all-embracing meaning of which we spoke earlier, and between instances of meaning-giving and the highest unity of meaning which is truth. What is seen in them is that all-embracing meaning – the highest unity of meaning – present *in* their meaning-giving and *in* the self-appropriation which occurs through it. Not that this is always true even of them: they *can* erroneously give meaning and mistake themselves. But *where* they are correct in assigning meaning to other people and things, the highest unity of meaning *is* anticipated in them, despite the habit in British religion of privatising the highest truth (God) in a remote 'place' distant from ordinary meaning-giving and personal self-appropriation.

This does not confer on these major figures the 'possession' of the truth, as though they themselves, or the particular instances of meaning-giving (meaning-claims) and self-appropriation which they accomplished, *contained* all-embracing meaning or the unity of truth as a property. What I am suggesting is that these emerge and become present *in* their meaning-giving and self-appropriation. Dangerous things happen when the all-embracing meaning or the unity of truth are *objectified* as properties of, rather than seen as emergent and present *in*, meaning-giving and self-appropriation. When such objectification occurs, the all-embracing meaning and truth are only vestigially present. For this reason, it is a dubious procedure to speak of 'experiences' or 'religious experiences'; this is in effect to stop the 'flow' of experience and meaning-giving and hypostatise an abstraction called 'an experience' which has the property of reference to, or presence of, the transcendent all-embracing meaning, rather than recognising that such all-embracing meaning *arises* in the active process of meaning-giving and self-appropriation *where* these are done appropriately.

The same problem occurs in many conventional ways of approaching traditional material. There have been repeated attempts to stabilise the presence of all-embracing meaning in the various religious traditions, which have led to immense diversities of claims and counter-claims. Now the same techniques have come to be used on 'religious traditions', and 'religions', 'dimensions', 'traditions', 'experiences', 'claims', 'stories', 'moral codes' and 'facts' have all been used to contain 'basic meaning'. But these are essentially objectifications, and abstractions. They may show people giving meaning, but only from an external standpoint; or they may assume that these *have* intrinsic meaning. How self-appropriation occurs through that is hardly apparent, and the presence of all-embracing truth – which by its nature cannot be confined in such limited situations – still less so.

Closely implicated in the failure of such stabilisations is the use of descriptive techniques and language, which cause the one approaching the religions, stories, behaviour and so on to adopt the position of a relatively passive observer who 'receives' the meaning which has been declared in the religions, stories, behaviour. He or she has this meaning done *for* him or her, and the meaning comes to him or her as 'given', and as a 'claim' which he can simply assimilate as information of an objective sort; exactly that may be expected by those who bring it. The meaning remains 'alien' in its objectivity even when he or she assimilates it – meaning 'put on' as learned or even understood, but not participated in. How does one participate in this meaning? This happens primarily through the *giving* of meaning, not by *being given* meaning, and by giving meaning in a way appropriate to that to which meaning is given; and through that giving we appropriate ourselves. It seems that we only do this fully when we become capable of articulating the meaning we give, and our self-appropriation – when we *produce* some appropriate tactile or symbolic expression (graphic, literary, or some other form).[12]

Descriptive presentations of those abstractions showing people giving meaning, proliferated out of a sense of responsibility to the many forms of life present in any one religious group and in many of them, run into a serious danger. They are superficially plausible, because people appear to take these presentations seriously; and in presenting them descriptively one satisfies a prime expectation in education, that for 'knowledge'. But in presenting many objectifications descriptively one provides little opportunity for self-appropriation through meaning-giving, and certainly one gives no opportunity for the expansion of that meaning which is necessary for an awareness of all-embracing meaning, or the ideal of truth, to be more than marginally present. In effect, both meaning and truth are lost by being disregarded in practice, as objectified units of meaning are described and handed over as knowledge. The more important task, self-appropriation in meaning-giving, is displaced in the anxiety to make people well-informed. Depth is sacrificed to the acquisition of a breadth of objective information learned-about, as the norms of modern education appear to require.

How then are the specific characteristics of past 'determinative' acts of meaning and self-appropriation, those which history has selected as anticipating the fullest truth, to enter the acts by which we now give meaning? If they do not come as objectified meanings which we assimilate as information and whose objective importance is commended to us as necessary to understanding, how are they to affect us? A satisfactory answer to this question is necessary if we are to progress beyond the insistence that education is primarily the learning of objective knowledge so that you can 'know about it' and be 'structured' by it. It is also necessary if we are to escape the inherent limitations of that 'learn and use' notion, its supposition that human beings naturally do (or should) repeat the same learned objective knowledge in each situation and repeatedly see each situation through the same knowledge. This notion is fundamentally mechanistic, and always breaks down in practice, because the advent of new situations questions the applicability of the learned objective knowledge. The 'given' knowledge is *strained* by the new, and is relativised; unless it can be adapted, it is at best retained as a 'possible knowledge' (what is often called a 'model' these days): that is, a form of knowledge which is only applicable in *some* situations. The notion and this dilemma bedevil modern understanding, as the increasing fragmentation of all knowledge and the many recent attempts to improve upon the 'learn and use' notion show.

Acts of meaning which history has selected as anticipating the fullest truth must enter our meaning-giving and self-appropriation by a primary *assent* on our part. This occurs when we *give them* meaning by being open to them in respect and trust, prepared to search them and understand them. In fact, the means by which we do this are wide-ranging – aesthetic, cognitive, behavioural and social; all, however, are a searching, active assent which attempts to accord with the historical acts of meaning while also *expanding* them (see page 105 above). The assent is expanded not *in vacuo*, as an act of historical fantasy, but in *our* meaning-giving and self-appropriation – that is, in the acts by which we accord meaning to our experience (see page 102 above) and appropriate ourselves anew by doing so. In other words, our assent to the historical acts of meaning is in our expansion of them in our own individual and social experience – by means of aesthetics, cognition, and behaviour. Furthermore, such assent in expansion actively makes the past *present*; and so there is no disjunction between past and present (see page 109 above).

Thus, in ordinary meaning given in experience, determinative acts of meaning from the past enter present meaning-giving. In general, their viability as 'determinative' rests on their continued use and expansion aesthetically, cognitively and behaviourally. So far as they show themselves capable of such presence and use, they remain determinative. By comparison with this, claiming a special position of authority for them, and sustaining this by coercive means, seem arbitrary and factually unjustified – bare 'truth-claims' for them based on *a priori* truth. But a claim for their special position as determinative which is made on the basis of their presence and use – that is, as an *a posteriori* judgement – is, of course, only a cognitive extension of their presence and use; as such, it would be legitimate, though abstract until accorded meaning by the hearer.

All this would be as applicable to Einstein or Darwin as to Muhammad or Jesus; all retain their viability as 'determinative' in continued use and expansion (and growth) in meaning-giving. Through their expansion in meaning-giving and self-appropriation, they become formative of, and anticipate, all-embracing meaning and the unity of truth. In the stages of their expansion – for example, in primitive understanding of each – they seem limited, but even then, relative to the particular stage, they seem to capture (if only hazily) the all-embracing meaning. Thus, at any particular stage, we see an aspect of limitation and also the *presence* in that limitation of the all-embracing meaning – a unity of particular and universal relative to that stage. To put it differently, we see their 'determinativeness' not only because of their continued use in expansion and growth, but because they are both 'limited' and (in their limitedness) 'opening'.

As 'opening', they seem not to confine us to seeing things in terms provided by a past 'act of meaning' but to open us to future 'acts of meaning', and to draw us onward to fuller meaning-giving. That is, they anticipate the completion of truth and also provide an ideal which 'claims' us for the truth. That they should do so is important: otherwise, there is no *necessity* to bring about a coherence among non-*religious* and *religious* 'determinative acts of meaning', *or* to bring about a coherence among various non-religious ones (for example, Einstein and Darwin), *or* to bring about a unity in various religious ones (for example, Muhammad and Jesus). Without the anticipation and ideal of a unity of truth, such coherence becomes *accidental*, depending on the presence of geographical factors (co-presence in the locality) or of cultural factors (say conventions about tolerance and mutual harmony).

And it is the responsibility laid upon us by being 'opened' and 'drawn' by the ideal of the completion of truth which requires us to judge amongst the many candidate 'determinatives'. This is a difficult task at the best of times, but it can be done if we take seriously our responsibility to anticipate that final completion or unity of truth by being drawn to fuller meaning-giving. In general, therefore, we shall judge candidates by their capacity to *continue* to anticipate the unity of truth by *expanding* in fuller meaning-giving and self-appropriation. This is to judge them by their past and continuing *durability*, a durability which has to include many different characteristics – aesthetic, cognitive, behavioural – and their appearance in comprehensive and well-structured forms which will make them applicable in the widest range of situations of meaning-giving and self-appropriation. Furthermore, they must incorporate means for their own dynamic and ongoing improvement; that is, they must themselves be both forward-looking and self-critical, drawn by the goal of the completion of a unity of truth.

Such criteria for selection amongst 'determinative acts of meaning' which are available as candidates will apply also in deciding upon their use in situations (such as education) where meaning-giving and self-appropriation are fostered. But it is very easy to take false steps in both selection and evaluation, through the uncritical employment of cultur-ally-transmitted prejudices, and in effect to *twist* our practices of mean-ing-giving and self-appropriation, those we employ for ourselves and commend to others. For example, the employment of a restricted idea of knowledge – what is sometimes called 'critical realism' – as central to life and education, leads to a form of life and education centred on a restricted form of meaning-giving and self-appropriation, one which tends to exclude the aesthetic and the behavioural in favour of a straightforward or modified form of the 'learning-using' notion (see page 111 above). The imposition of this idea of knowledge as normative provokes counter-claims from those concerned with wider forms of meaning-giving and self-appropriation, either by claiming a 'higher form' of critical realism (the notion of revelation is often used this way in theology) which has many of the same restrictions as found in ordinary critical realism, or by claiming the need for aesthetic and moral forms of meaning-giving as necessary to personal development.

The results of such situations are false divisions manifested in policy and/or practice, as can quickly be seen in British and American education, for example, where culturally-reinforced norms have often created an education which is an homogeneous form of critical realism, while other forms of meaning-giving have been allowed only on sufferance (as a prag-matic compromise), or have retreated to places or institutions where they can expand unchallenged. An additional problem is that those who have succeeded in claiming a position for wider forms of meaning-giving in the same institutions (where critical realism is normative) frequently adopt modified norms of the same kind as those employed by the critical realists. That is, they retain the supposition that education *is* centrally concerned with objective knowledge of the kind supposed to exist in the natural sciences, and therefore attempt to justify their work on *those* educational grounds. Following this, they permit themselves only the task of inform-ing people about ways by which *others* find meaning, in effect making human ways of finding meaning into the objective knowledge which is to be 'learned and used'. Correspondingly, they develop their own rationale for their work, using the educational grounds of critical realism in doing so, with the added suggestion that there should be 'the provision of oppor-tunities for pupils to reflect about themselves, their relationships and the wider world'.[13] This is seen, for example, in current British religious edu-cation, where there is a self-generated 'educational' rationale for the sub-ject, developed in sharp contradistinction from church or theological rationales.

But if our task is to be responsible as we are 'drawn' and 'opened' by the ideal of the completion of truth, such norms and rationales, as well as the divisions which result from them, need to be seen in that light. So seen, they appear as attempts to anticipate the fullest truth, but as sharply limited both in themselves and in what they produce. That conclusion is supported in a variety of ways, by the general advance beyond critical realism in the sciences, philosophy and religious thought, by the recognition of the centrality of meaning and personal self-appropriation, and by the desire for a more advanced understanding of the coherence of all meaning-giving. And this is no retreat into vagueness; there is as much concern as ever for all meaning-giving to be engaged in critically, taking up the 'acts of meaning' of Einstein, Darwin, Muhammad and Jesus and others in an expansion which is also a critical anticipation of the unity of truth.

Does any party have special access to the final unity of truth, whether they be scientist, artist, philosopher, ethicist or theologian, so that they can provide us with clear and timeless norms about truth? No. Though we may and should attempt to speak universally, the meaning that we give – and the meaning that we find in giving it – is always particular to a place and time, and accommodated to our various capacities and situation as a further expansion of determinative acts of meaning. It will have greater value as it overcomes the limitations and divisions which constantly occur in what we do, until finally the truth appears fully in our acts of meaning and we find ourselves in truth. It is the task of all people, all educators and all religions and theologians, to bring this about.

So far as we do already give meaning *correctly* (and appropriate ourselves in doing so), even in our limitations, and thus anticipate the unity of truth, the truth is *already* in what we do and are, both as individuals and in social relationships (such as teaching). That is what frees us to understand the world, each other and ourselves and to go on to do so more fully. It is that *active ideal*, already present in our meaning-giving and self-appropriation, which *some* of us call the Spirit of the God and Father of Jesus Christ.

To think it, speak it, live it thus – as the Spirit of God and Father of Jesus Christ – is of course a particular way of 'establishing' the determinative act of meaning which is expanded and as such enters, apparently inexhaustibly, into the meaning-giving and self-appropriation of those who use this particular way. It is also a particular way of construing the presence of the all-embracing meaning and the unity of truth to which they look forward. To engage in such particular ways, whether monotheistic and Jewish, Christian, or Muslim, or non-monotheistic and Hindu, or non-theistic and Buddhist, is necessary to apprehending, comprehending and living as a human being. However, if such are treated as the norms for all they become divisive, and the same problems arise as when the critical realist notion of knowledge is treated as normative. Each might generate authoritarianism of a comprehensive kind *unless* recognised as itself a giving of a particular meaning, a necessary 'accommodation' to human sensibility, understanding and action – though none the less, *if correct*, it is a presence of the ultimate unity of truth. In other words, each must be recognised as contingent in its thinkability and livability but if correct as a presence of the ultimate.

How are these apparently incompatible particularities to be brought together without losing their value as particular meaning-giving, and without giving one or some of them a position of dominance? How is this to be done for religious, and not only geographical or cultural, reasons? (*That* it should be done is a responsibility which arises from anticipation of the unity of truth: see page 112 above.) It is to be done, fundamentally, by that primary act of assent mentioned earlier (page 111), whereby we, standing in one 'particularity', give to another meaning by being open to it in respect and trust, seeking to expand our meaning-giving by searching and understanding the other by all appropriate means, and then freshly appropriating our own identity through that process. What occurs thereby is a *progressive* and *dynamic realisation* of the unity of truth *in* the meaning given to another particularity, which – again, *if correct* – is a presence of the ultimate 'between' the particular ways. Personal commitment in one 'way' is thus preserved and enlarged through meaning given to the other 'way', and the self established in giving. 'Whosoever will save his life shall lose it; but whosoever shall lose his life for my sake and the gospel's, the same shall save it' (Mark 8: 35). Of course, some religions and non-religions are not up to this task; they will remain insular, and will eventually fail.

References

1 Birmingham Agreed Syllabus of Religious Instruction, page 4.
2 Cf. TRACY, DAVID (1981) *The Analogical Imagination.* New York: Crossroad Press.
3 BALTHASAR, HANS URS VON (1967) *The God Question and Modern Man.* New York: Seabury Press (38 ff.).
4 WELTE, B. (1965) *Auf der Spur des Ewigen.* (20).
5 LONERGAN, BERNARD (1980) *Understanding and Being.* New York: Edwin Mellen Press (189).
6 RASHKE, CARL A. (1982) 'The deconstruction of God', in *Deconstruction and Theology.* New York: Crossroad Press (8).
7 Ibid., page 9.
8 DELEUZE, GILLES (1983) *Nietzsche and Philosophy.* London: Athlone Press (98).
9 HICK, JOHN H. (1973) *God and the Universe of Faiths.* London: Macmillan.
  SMART, NINIAN (1973) *The Religious Experience of Mankind.* London: Collins (Fontana).
10 SCHUON, FRITHJOF (1975) *Logic and Transcendence.* New York: Harper and Row (Torchbooks).
11 PANNENBERG, WOLFHART (1976) *Basic Questions in Theology*, Vol. II. London: SCM Press (21).
12 Cf. SCHOLES, ROBERT (1982) *Semiotics and Interpretation.* New Haven, CT: Yale University Press.
13 *Education: Principles in Religious Education.* London: British Council of Churches (n.d.) (1)

A Response to Daniel W. Hardy

Anza A. Lema

I am grateful to the Revd D. W. Hardy for his presentation. He has talked
at length on concepts of an all-embracing meaning of life, of consciousness, and of the truth. I may have some problems here and there to follow
some of the arguments – but lack of agreement is not always a bad thing.
In fact, I tend to believe that some of my problems arise from the fact that I
come from a different social and cultural background and that my thought
patterns, through which I describe and judge the world I live in, are
different from his. I have no problem, for instance, in equating Truth
with the Being, the Will or the Word of God. In that sense, truth does
have for me the highest unity of meaning. I believe that society is served
by truth. There is, therefore, a need for educators and theologians to stand
up for truth as they see it. However, I find that it becomes more meaningful when the basis of that truth is found in my cultural context; otherwise truth becomes an elusive idea. For the whole truth cannot be known
to any of us; we may have stumbled on a new part of it, but we must not
assume more.

If I were to choose one particular cultural approach as determinative of
my whole understanding of human being, then I shall, presumably, adopt
an unrealistic view of human life as a whole. I appreciate Mr. Hardy's
warning that human motivation and human capacity to comprehend what
he calls 'an all-embracing' meaning of life are hardly ever what they seem.
For our conscious actions and reactions are only one part of us and not
necessarily the determining part of us. We have to allow, not only for
subjectivity, but for the fact that our subjectivity, our judgements tend to
be shaped by that which is not known to us and of which we may not be
aware. We are left, therefore, with evidence of confusion about the
meaning of the whole of life and with questions about the validity of
human judgements.

One more important point may be made here. It is the Word of God which says, 'the truth shall make you free'. Jesus says: 'I am the way, the truth and the life.' Today we talk a lot about scientific truth, and there is, indeed, such a thing as scientific evidence. However, scientific evidence is not the sort of evidence which, of itself, establishes an overview. Scientific evidence describes what it describes and cannot go any further to provide that which Mr. Hardy has termed the all-embracing meaning of life.

Education and Theology

It is indeed true that theologians and educators have a special contribution to make to the search and development of truth in our world. But it is important for all of us to realise the fact that searching for truth does not mean working in a vacuum. Theologians and educators are all dependent upon the society of which they are members. They therefore need to be committed members of their society and devise their research and other work for the service of that society. It would be grossly arrogant for anyone to speak the truth as one sees it regardless of the consequences for society.

The purpose of education and theology must be to serve the development of society or they lose their credibility. The objective of that development is the people – to create the kind of conditions, both material and spiritual, which enable them as individuals and as communities to enhance their well-being and preserve their human dignity. It is a development which involves economic, political and social justice.

Education in its fullest sense should be integrative. It should seek to develop each dimension of human life, physical, aesthetic, intellectual, psychological and spiritual. Furthermore, the knowledge of each dimension should be brought into a unitary programme. By the same token, teaching and learning should have as their major objective the prime development of the individual – in other words, of human life. For, indeed, people can be taught and learn for lopsided development, for limitation, distortion and even destruction of human life and its environment. The way in which people respond to and act upon the world can be seen as an indicator of the content and quality of their consciousness. And the development of human consciousness is to a very large extent an educational responsibility.

The Christian perspective on education is determined by what the Christian believes about the person of God, the destiny of man, the nature of the world and the mission of the church. Admittedly, among Christians there are a number of different interpretations of these theological cornerstones, but it is from this basic level that a distinctively Christian approach to education must be built up. In this regard, one of the most stimulating discussions for Christians involved in any aspect of education is the theological interpretation developed by Nels S. Ferré in his book, *A Theology for Christian Education*. In the experience of people today, he suggests, God is known most significantly as Educator. For humankind, then, God's world, including the evil, suffering and death which are an integral part of life, is 'a pedagogical process for learning to know God's love and to live in it'. Christ, in his life, death and resurrection, becomes the Christian's great 'Exemplar, God's concrete educational demonstration not only of what life is all about but also of the way to learn' the life of love. The Holy Spirit is then understood as God's Tutor, who 'takes the things of Christ' and leads us into all truth, who 'uses world history and nature as the general education that prepares for the fuller school of Christ within the Christian community'.[1] Humanity has been created with the capacity and the opportunity to learn that their true destiny as human beings is fulfilled only as they learn to live a life of love and service to the world, as true sons and daughters of God.

Whether or not we fully accept such an interpretation, we need to recognise that it highlights a number of truths concerning the Christian attitude to education. First, there is the fundamental acknowledgment that it is God who educates his children, whether it be informally through the experiences of life or through the more structured activities of a church educational programme. It is God's love alone that nourishes and nurtures our early growth in the Christian faith, that challenges and strengthens us in our striving for Christian maturity.[2]

Christian Truth and the World

Christian educators cannot ignore or withdraw from the world, which is not only God's creation but the object of his reconciling love and the medium through which he educates his people. 'The true church in its educational ministry,' declared Father Aram Keshishian, in a sermon at the Glion Consultation on Sunday School work in Europe, '. . .is called to cope with the challenges of the world and the demands of the pluralistic societies. The church must respond with new vision in courage and humility and with an attempt at deeper understanding of conflicting situations; it has to respond to it as a calling rather than as a task, as a promise rather than as a threat. All the challenging possibilities I believe will open new and promising horizons in the mission of the church for a greater and wider experience of God in the world and will give fresh insight and impetus to its involvement in the service of God to the world.'[3]

At different times there have been those in the church who have assumed the authority to lord it over all other forms of knowledge and proclaim that the doctrines of the church and the Bible as the revealed Word of God constituted the only knowledge a man needed to learn. Such people have had a view of an all-powerful and all-knowing God who fills the empty vessels of his people with his knowledge, thus limiting their freedom and responsibility for action in the world. This kind of approach has almost always been associated with the church's withdrawal from the world. Christian congregations have been developed as holy fortresses where the faithful believers could take refuge from the wickedness and temptations of the world.

Many who argue for church schools today appeal to the need to protect growing children from the decadence of the present generation. The danger is that in such a hothouse atmosphere Christians are never exposed to the demands of God to serve the world, nor able to grow to Christian maturity by testing the adequacy of their faith against the realities of life. When the church concentrates its educational efforts in this way, exclusively in building up a faithful elite to be kept holy and pure from the defilement of contact with the world, the church is in fact denying its Lord and the whole meaning of his incarnation and crucifixion.

Those who accept that the Christian's place is in the world have a creative freedom and God-given responsibility to live out the Christian faith in the context of their particular society and culture and to relate the Christian truths about life to all other forms of truth and knowledge. They recognise that there are different sorts of truth. One thing may be demonstrated experimentally, another proved logically necessary, a third may be personally experienced. All three are true, but in quite different ways, according to quite different criteria. The sort of knowledge represented by accurate recall and repetition is quite different from what is involved in perceptive observation, understanding a new idea or another person's state of mind, a flash of insight or the interpretation of a piece of poetry or music. None of these forms of truth is more valid or significant than the others. They represent different approaches to truth, each of which is peculiarly appropriate to a particular field of knowledge and quite inappropriate outside this realm. Once this is recognised, there is no difficulty in accepting the fact that the truth of the Christian faith is not the sort that can be scientifically demonstrated or logically deduced, but rather is concerned with the ultimate meaning of life that can only be understood and interpreted through personal experience. Yet, it is intimately related to all other realms of knowledge, for the Christian acknowledges God as the one in whom all things unite and find their true meaning and purpose. Such an approach gives rise to the paradoxical truth that the Christian 'knows all things only in God' and 'God in all things'.

The churches' involvement in education today is certainly full of challenges and problems. In the process of finding our way through the current difficulties, adapting old patterns or developing new forms of education which truly express the central truths of Christianity in the context of the twentieth century, we cannot do better than return again and again to the words of St Paul and ponder their implications for individual and community education within God's world; '. . .each of us has been given his gift, his due portion of Christ's bounty. . . And these were his gifts: some to be apostles, some prophets, some evangelists, some pastors and teachers, to equip God's people for work in his service, to the building up of the body of Christ. So shall we all at last attain to the unity inherent in our faith and our knowledge of the Son of God – to mature manhood, measured by nothing less than the full stature of Christ' (Ephesians 4: 7, 11-13, NEB).

References

1 FERRE, NELS F. S. (1969) *A Theology for Christian Education*. Phila-
   delphia, PA: Westminster Press (pp. 210–11).
2 Ibid., p. 110.
3 KESHISHIAN, ARAM (1973) *SSCCEE Official Report*, Document 3,
   Morning Service 28 September 1973.

On Acknowledging Religious Pluralism in Education

Johannes Lähnemann

The Situation

The situation is determined by the fact that we live in a multicultural and multireligious society – in West Germany and West Berlin as well as in the other states of Western Europe. The development is very rapid, especially in West Germany and West Berlin. For example, in West Berlin in 1959 there were only 200 Turks. In 1971 there were 54,000 and now there are about 120,000 Turks (that means evey second foreigner in the city); 12 per cent of the whole population of West Berlin are now of foreign extraction. Especially important for our theme is the increasing number of Muslim children; in Germany, these now approach half a million. In spite of the restrictions on new foreign workers, many of their dependants have come to Germany, and very many 'foreign' children are, of course, born in West Germany. By 1985 every tenth child in West German schools will be a Muslim. As a consequence, in the big cities there may be up to 40 per cent or more schoolchildren from Muslim families.

There is not only an increasing number of religious minorities with which to contend, there is also the increasing secularity of society at large.

A now newly arriving Muslim will very often feel no more 'strange' in Western Europe than a practising Catholic or Protestant Christian facing the materialistic values of our technological civilisation.[1]

The main danger is the loss of religious (or philosophical) and ethical orientation in a period which requires of human beings a developed ethical conscience to cope with all the difficult questions of survival and harmonious living.

There are three special dangers if the cultural and religious education of Muslim *and* Christian children is not improved. The first danger is the loss of religious and ethical orientation for most of the young 'foreign' people, with a consequent uncritical accommodation to the materialistic values of our technological civilisation. The second, and opposite, danger is that young foreigners especially will follow the religious and politically radical groups which use the democratic system to be active in a way they could never be in their home countries. The third danger is that the German population will treat all foreigners as a threat to their own cultural civilisation and wealth.

In addition to the large number of foreign pupils, there is an increasing number of foreign teachers in German schools. While this is a valuable aid for the foreign pupils, their presence also brings about a number of new problems.

First, most of these foreign teachers have too little knowledge of the German language. Many of them come to Germany without being intensively trained in the subject, and so they have difficulties in communicating with German teachers and in benefitting from post-graduate training programmes for teaching children of migrant workers. Hence they are unable to give lessons in Islamic religious education in the German language. It is just this which is important if Muslim children are to develop a Muslim identity *within* German society.

Secondly, the foreign teachers have hardly any knowledge of the cultural, religious and historical background of West German society. For example, a good friend of mine, a Turkish teacher with a German paedogogical diploma and a good knowledge of the German language, had observed the interest of his pupils in religious questions. So he decided to talk to them about Muslim and Christian feasts. He tried to compare the *Kurban Bayram* – the great feast with the sacrifice of animals during the days of the Mecca pilgrimage – with the Christian Christmas. He said:

> Christians too have a sacrifice at Christmas. They cut the Christmas tree. Isn't that also a kind of sacrifice?

Clearly he did not know much about the central meaning of Christmas and could misinterpret a recent and local Christian custom as the fundamental act at Christmas.

While foreign teachers have difficulties with German culture, German teachers very rarely have any idea of the cultural, religious and historical backgrounds of the children of migrant workers. Again, here is an example. At the beginning of a teacher-training seminar in Lüneburg we had a brain-storming session about Islam. It was striking what preconceptions the students expressed concerning this religion – for example, that it is fanatical as well as fatalistic, that it is a religion which suppresses women, and that Muhammad, in contrast to Jesus, could not be recognised as a serious religious figure.

Finally, only very seldom are German and foreign teachers able to co-operate. This is due not only to lack of knowledge about each other but also to the fact that the training of teachers in the home countries of immigrants is very different from that found in West Germany. The foreign teachers are not used to the German way of working with curricula and with open forms of teaching.

The Aim

The aim of living together harmoniously requires that we do not see the proximity of different cultures as a threat to the identity of either, but as an opportunity for the enrichment of our horizons and experience. It follows that it will not be adequate just to give special help to foreign children.

It is necessary that the whole of life in school and in society becomes open for the meeting of cultures. Accordingly, the aim for religious and cultural education should be two-fold: to enable children to have a better knowledge of the religious and cultural background from which they come, and at the same time to develop a welcoming acceptance of, and interest in, other cultures and religions. All children need a better understanding of their own roots in a particular religion and culture, and at the same time a perspective for the future which enables them to appreciate the values that have led to the formulation of fundamental human rights. They also need a better understanding of the values and 'way of life' of the children who do not belong to their own confession or religion. This does not mean restricting the ordinary offering of religious education in schools, but intensifying and opening it up to questions raised by the meeting of cultures. But still more is needed. We should aim for the co-ordination of educational activities toward such an inter-cultural encounter both in school *and* in other educational institutions in society. We should foster better contacts between theological and general religious research, nurturing a dialogue between religions (and philosophical systems), particularly in practical religious and cultural life. For instance, at the moment there is very little dialogue between traditional Protestant theology in Germany and the general discipline of religious study.

At the moment, Protestant theology in Germany is mainly concerned with its own history and theological tradition, with biblical research, and with discussing the challenges of a secular society. Only seldom have world religions become a theological theme – as a challenge for the articulation of Christian truth in a world-wide context and for the development of a dialogue between cultures and religions. The situation in Great Britain is more encouraging; there general religious research appears more often to be a theme for theologians than it is in Germany. The existence of such research, or lack of it, will have consequences for the nature of religious education. In the training of teachers for religious education and of church ministers in West Germany, the study of non-Christian religions is traditionally little more than a hobby. Consequently, you will find very few pages on world religions in traditional German schoolbooks. There are only some short stories, or a (mostly inaccurate) summary of the doctrines of other religions.[2] A very popular story tells how a man fell

down a well and needed help to get out again. Confucius passed by and
said to him:
'If you had followed my doctrines you would never have fallen down
there.'
Buddha came along and said:
'You must learn that all life is suffering.'
Muhammad arrived and shouted:
'Help yourself. Then God will help you.'
At last Jesus came, climbed down into the well, held the man in his arms
and brought him up again. It is true that the way of Jesus is the way of
helping suffering people, but the descriptions of the actions of the other
religious figures shows that there is no real appreciation of the experiences, the values, the life and the philosophy of the other great religions.

Still worse was the instruction about other religions which was sometimes found in history and geography books. In a school geography, for
example, the only pictures about Hindu life in India showed the worship
of cows and the giving of food to rats in a temple, and on the opposite page
a photograph of a starving man in the streets of Calcutta. There was no
hint of the different conception of the structures of life and of the different
way all creatures belong together as living souls according to Hindu
doctrine.

I should now like to try to give an idea of what could be done in different
fields in the encounter between religions. I shall be mainly concerned
with the relationship between Christians and Muslims because Islam
constitutes the largest religious minority in West Germany and the
United Kingdom, and because there are special problems between these
two religions arising from their long history as 'neighbours'.

The Task

The aim of living together harmoniously requires the carrying out of a
multiplicity of tasks, because enounter between religions is a complex
process. It involves

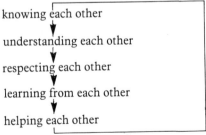

One step leads to the next. It is not necessary that intellectual learning
should be the starting point. Very often the practical challenge of living
together will bring out the questions necessary for a better understanding
of one another. Clearly the intellectual dimension is essential, but the

emotional and the practical are necessary as well. The whole person should be involved, from head (the brain) to foot (the process of visiting each other).

The encounter between religions is a process for both sides. It is not simply for the one to give, the other to receive. Both religions are going to find a new way of life and new possibilities for the articulation of their values in the secular context of living. It should be clear that this is a long and difficult way. You cannot within the space of a few months or even a few years change the consciousness of living beside another and living against another which has developed over centuries.

The Encounter between Religions in the Different Fields and in the Context of Education

THE SOCIAL DIMENSION

All education depends upon a context of living together in families, in neighbourhoods, in communities, in which the willingness to learn from each other is to be developed. (On the other hand, living together in communities must be supported by systematic instruction in schools and among the different religious groupings.) This can be demonstrated by the example of a West German suburb where a Protestant congregation was confronted with a total change in the nature of the population in its part of the town. In the kindergarten, for example, teachers suddenly had to deal with children from eight different nations. How were they to cope with the fear Turkish parents had of the 'free' climate in German educational institutions? How were the Turks to cope with German prejudices against the 'heathens'? The way forward was found by a common celebration of festivals which were prepared by Germans and Turks together and which have subsequently led to a wide range of common activities, including religious dialogue and special forms of common worship.

The common celebration of festivals destroyed walls of prejudice and opened the way for religious dialogue. It is a new experience for Christians, in that they are not confronted by secular or unbelieving people but by those for whom piety plays a central role in daily life. The idea of a worship service celebrated by Christians *and* Muslims was the result of many talks over a long period. The first experiment took place on *Muttertag* ('Mother's day') which is celebrated in Turkey as well as in Germany. The theme was, 'We make time for one another, because it's great to have a family.' It was not a mixture of Christian and Muslim worship. Each side was responsible for that part of worship which it had prepared, and in which the other side took part as 'guests'. After a year of meetings and common celebrations, life together in that suburb has taken on a new dimension which both sides would not now wish to lose.[3]

THE THEOLOGICAL DIMENSION

My intention here is to show that both religions already have in themselves the motivation to recognise believers of other religions not only as human beings but also as creatures of God with their own values and virtues demanding respect.

> The ethical content of Islam embraces all the virtues professed by all righteous members of mankind, including even those who may not believe in a personal God.[4]

And these are Jesus's words in the parable of the last judgement (Matthew 25: 40):

> Verily I say unto you, inasmuch as ye have done it unto one of the least of these my brethren, ye have done it unto me.

('It', according to Matthew 25: 35, means:

> For I was an hungred, and ye gave me meat; I was thirsty, and ye gave me drink; I was a stranger, and ye took me in; naked, and ye clothed me; I was sick, and ye visited me, I was in prison, and ye came unto me.)

A central theme in the Gospels is that Jesus opens up the limits of the Jewish confession because the love of God he brings cannot be restricted to a particular group of people. This love also includes the enemy, and those of other nations and confessions, as can be illustrated, for example, by the parable of the good Samaritan.

Of course, there are also essential differences between Christian and Muslim belief: believing in Jesus Christ as *the* saviour of all mankind on the one side, believing in the Qur'ān as *the* external word of God on the other. It is typical that according to St John's Gospel, 'the Word was made *flesh*' (John 1: 14), while a Muslim would say that the Word of God was made *book*. This has important consequences for the understanding of the 'holy scriptures', for the understanding of salvation, for the understanding of prophecy and many other theological themes. Especially important is the difference in the understanding of humankind as essentially sinful in Christianity, in contrast to the more optimistic anthropology of Islam. Yet I suggest that there is not one theological theme in either religion where one cannot come to a better understanding of the other, at least by clearing away misunderstanding and prejudice.

To give just one example, there is the Muslim reading of the Christian doctrine of the Trinity as a form of believing in three gods. Here one should explain that the doctrine of the Trinity mainly describes the incredible love of God in Jesus Christ who came to mankind and especially to the lost. There is, on the other hand, the Christian view of Allah as a God of despotic arbitrariness, which does not correspond to the Qur'ānic view of a God of mercy. Providing an historical point of view can be especially helpful: on one side, to show that the title 'God's Son' in early Christianity would never mean the idea of a physical son, and on the other, Muslim, side, to show that the doctrine of Allah's 'attributes' has some analogy with the Christian doctrine of the Trinity.[5]

There are many doctrinal similarities and parallel structures of worship in the two religions. Their discovery can help us to better understanding and co-operation: being thankful for God's creation, the calling to an unselfish life, working for righteousness, being responsible for all creatures, helping the weak, to mention only some of the major common themes of Islam and Christianity. Furthermore, one can say that Christians in some instances can learn from Muslims, and Muslims can learn from Christians. Muslims very often give a splendid example of faithfulness in following their religious task, and display an attitude of devotion to God which implies steadiness, calmness, and a great responsibility for family, neighbourhood, guests and strangers. On the other hand, Muslims can find in Christian churches a great responsibility in social affairs which is derived from the commandment of love. Many Christian groups have, for example, devoted a great deal of imagination to the creation of a common life for healthy and handicapped people – a life which has its source in God's love as it is revealed in Jesus Christ.

Meeting in Schools

The prejudices dividing Christians from Muslims, the product of a long history, call for much educational work in schools as well as in society and in theology. This cannot be done by religious instruction alone. Pupils need a better knowledge of history, cultural development, forms of life, and also information about the political and economic implications and out-workings of religion. Subjects such as history, geography, social and political instruction all need to be drawn in to give young people an idea of the complexity of religious development. It is, for example, important to overcome the kind of history lesson which is mainly a description of wars and conflicts and which does not lead to a better understanding of the 'neighbourhood' of the religions and the mutual cultural influences. But in schools learning and living should go together. It is important to look out for opportunities to meet people, and especially children from other cultural backgrounds, to hear from them about their customs, and to tell them about one's own culture and religion. The presence of children of different religions and nations is a challenge for the whole of school life (for example, through common celebrations of the main festival days of the religions).

In her article 'Islam in the Primary School', Elizabeth Wilson has described in a very sensitive way what one might do with young children concerning Islam. She writes: 'Our aim must. . .be not to teach Islam, how could we, but to help children adopt attitudes that are sensitive and creative, to realise that love, sympathy and integrity are values cherished by Christianity and Islam and are found expressed in the lives of people of all faiths and may be found in the homes of children everywhere.'[6] And she proposes that school assemblies 'might well include from time to time a short passage from the Bible and a complementary one from the Qur'ān, possibly read by one of the Muslim children. . . It is important that in the school community, all make their contribution by sharing their prayers, pictures, models and music.'

Special Tasks and Opportunities of Religious Instruction

The special tasks and opportunities of religious instruction in schools should follow the general aim (see page 123 above) in a specifically systematic way. The concept of religious education in a multicultural society is more developed in the United Kingdom than it is in Germany. This is mainly to the credit of the Shap Working Party on World Religions in Education which has brought forward a number of quality publications and a great deal of educational work. There is a respectable number of publications from authors such as John R. Hinnels, Eric J. Sharpe, Ninian Smart, E.G. Parrinder, Owen Cole, John Shepherd, Jean Holm, to mention only some of them. One of the basic books is *Comparative Religion in Education*, a collection of studies edited by J.R. Hinnels.[7] It is a fact that the experiences of the meeting of cultures have a longer history in Great Britain, not least because of the heritage of the Commonwealth. To understand the situation in West Germany one must know that there is separate religious instruction for Protestant and Roman Catholic children, and in some places also for Jewish children (in accordance with Article 7 of the Federal German Republic's constitution, *Grundgesetz*). Pupils who do not belong to one of these religious communities, or whose parents do not want them to attend this confessional teaching, should attend alternative lessons, which are known by different names in the different *Lands* of the Federal Republic, for example, 'ethical instruction'. The curricula for confessional teaching have to be worked out according to the doctrines of the respective churches, and of the Jewish community, but also of course according to the principles of the constitution and the general aims of the public (state) schools in the various *Lands*.

It is therefore my impression that in West Germany it is easier to follow the first part of the general aim – 'to enable children to have a better knowledge of their own religion and culture' – while in Great Britain there is a greater stock of experience concerning the second part – 'to develop a welcoming acceptance of, and interest in, another culture and religion'. What we need in West Germany is, first, to institute a regular form of religious instruction for Muslim children, and secondly, to open the confessional (Protestant and Roman Catholic) religious instruction to the question raised by the meeting of cultures. I shall try to give examples of both.

    1 The development of a curriculum for religious instruction for Muslim children in public (state) schools in North Rhine-

Westphalia (with aims which are open to an encounter between religions, and which face the challenges presented by the values of our industrial civilisation).

2 A survey of aims for Protestant religious instruction in encountering Islam for pupils of different age groups which I have formulated in my book *Nichtchristliche Religionen im Unterricht*.[8] (See Appendixes A and B, pages 130–4.)

Religious and Cultural Values in Teacher-training

One cannot enable children to have a better knowledge of, and an open interest in, other religions and cultures if teachers have no basic instruction in the field. It will not be sufficient for teacher trainees in the field of religion to attend one or two seminars in this subject so long as the students of history, geography, and social and political sciences are not prepared to co-operate. So *all* teachers should, for example, be aware of the heritage of the Islamic culture of the Middle Ages, or the post-colonial situation in the Middle East, and, not least, of the reasons for the migration of labour in our time. This should be recognised in training projects for all teachers, and especially in those for teachers of religion, and for teachers of children of migrant workers. Foreign teachers, Muslims especially, in their turn need a better knowledge of the history of Europe, the history and doctrines of Christianity, the Age of Enlightenment, and the origins of the industrial revolution.

In conclusion, I should like to outline some of the training projects for the teachers of migrant workers' children which are developing in West Germany, and to introduce a plan of my own (see Appendix C, pages 135–6) which might be discussed in the light of experiences and possibilities in other countries of Western Europe. At different universities, and also in most of the ministries for cultural and public instruction, there is now an understanding of the need to offer special training for the teaching of children of migrant workers. For example, in Bavaria the regulations for the examination of teachers provide for the possibility of post-graduate training in teaching German as a foreign language to immigrant children. There are courses of study for teachers of foreign children in several universities and teacher-training colleges – in Bremen, in Giessen, in Kassel, in Landau in co-operation with the University of Mainz, and at three teacher-training colleges in Baden-Württemberg: Karlsruhe, Schwäbisch Gmünd, and Weingarten. At other universities comparable courses of study are planned – for example, in Hamburg, Oldenburg and Nürnberg. The main subject of all these courses is language, German as well as foreign language. Indeed, language is in many ways the door which enables foreign children to enter German society, and for teachers to understand the problems of these children and their families. But as regards religious education, there is in these projects far too little space in the curriculum for an introduction to the culture, history and religion of the countries of origin of foreign workers.

Frequently, there is no more than a weekly two-hour seminar over one term to introduce students to the situation in the country of origin. Moreover, there is one important deficiency: only at Kassel is there the opportunity for German and foreign teachers to take part in a joint course of study.

I should like to see a strengthening of the project by the Goethe-Institute to give foreign teachers an intensive introduction to the German language in their home countries before they come to Germany so that they are able to attend and benefit from post-graduate training courses in Germany. These courses of study in turn should contain a larger proportion of elements which may be taken jointly by German and foreign teachers. Moreover, they should contain additional options specifically for foreign and for German teachers separately tailored to their specific needs. It is, of course, assumed that practical work in schools and the practical development of curricula should be a constituent part of these studies.

Appendix A

THE TASKS OF ISLAMIC RELIGIOUS EDUCATION (a teaching framework)

1 *Assumptions and aims*

Religious education classes for pupils of Islamic faith living in the Federal German Republic take place in certain circumstances. There are some specific implications for this school subject which follow from these circumstances. Muslims in Germany live in an unfamiliar cultural environment. Coming to terms with real-life situations, and the development of long-term prospects for living in German society, can often cause considerable stress because of the different degree of social progress, and the different relationship of religion to culture, society and politics from that of their own country. In addition, linguistic, social and economic problems are features of everyday life for the majority of people who come to look for work in Germany.

For the children there are additional problems. Frequently they know their own culture only from stories and from the daily habits of their parents, not from personal observation of life in the country of origin of their families. For Turkish Muslims there is a further factor: for more than fifty years their society has been undergoing fundamental change in the political, economic and cultural, and therefore inevitably also in the religious, sphere. The values, attitudes, patterns of behaviour and conduct brought from their own country do not always correspond with the exigencies of life in Germany; often they are a cause of uncertainty instead of providing the confidence to associate with Germans, their society and their culture. This tension will necessarily be greater when the belief in values brought to Germany has already been shaken by recent historical events in their home country.

By dint of living together and working together new patterns are slowly formed on both sides, capable of bringing the different cultures closer together. More significantly, for the generation of Muslim children born in Germany, the two cultures meet during the process of the individual development of the young people: on the one hand, education and everyday life within the family with its traditional values and patterns of behaviour, on the other, the world of work of their parents, and not least the mass media. If Muslims and non-Muslims, Turks and Germans, are to live and work together in Germany peacefully and constructively for the benefit of all, such a bicultural socialisation should not be expected to happen simply of its own accord.

In this context, religious education has a specific task:
- to contribute to the greater understanding by the generations of Muslims born in Germany of their own Islamic tradition, its history, ethics and faith, and by means of this tradition to give a sense of direction to the individual;
- to contribute to the development of an Islamic identity in a non-Muslim environment;
- to contribute to a better life together between Turks and Germans, Muslims and Christians, in equality, peace, and mutual respect.

This means that religious education for children of Islamic faith should take account of their situation in Germany; Islamic tradition must make it possible to explain, and to come to terms with, the life of Muslims in Germany. This means that Islam must be prepared to answer questions that have not, before now, been asked in the country of origin. There must be a clear link between Islamic tradition and the reality of life for Muslims in West German society. This also means that the values and attributes of both cultures must be related to each other, that the incompatible, as well as the compatible, nature of issues should be clearly revealed through open, frank discussion, and so further the efforts for harmony through mutual learning.

This imposes heavy demands on the teacher. On the one hand he or she must relate Islamic tradition to the social conditions prevailing in the Federal German Republic. On the other hand, he or she must interpret, in the light of the Islamic tradition, the experiences which the pupils have daily of these social conditions so that support in coming to terms with life may emerge.

2 *Content structure*

	EVERYDAY LIFE IN GERMANY		FOUNDATIONS OF ISLAM
	Experiencing and learning about the environment	Duties, Worship and	Religious knowledge
Class 1	1 'We get to know each other in religious education classes.' 2 'Our family.'	3 'We celebrate festivals.' 4 'Cleanliness is part of religion.'	5 'We learn about Muhammad and the Qur'ān.' 6 'The mosque –our house of prayer.'
Class 2	7 'We live in a strange environment.' 8 'Allah wants all men to work.'	9 'We must be honest.' 10 'Ramadan and our time of fasting.'	11 'Muhammad, the Prophet.' 12 'Learning about Allah.'
Class 3	Friendship Community	Purity Charity Pilgrimage	Muhammad, the Imam
	PROJECT TITLES		
Class 4	Turks/Muslims – a minority in Germany Other religions	Islamic virtues Prayer	Knowledge of the Qur'ān Five pillars
	PROJECT TITLES		

From the proposals *Religious Education for Pupils of Islamic Faith*, twelve teaching units, Landesinstitut für Curriculum-entwicklung (State Centre for Curriculum Development).[9]

Appendix B

AIMS FOR THE TEACHING OF ISLAM IN PROTESTANT RELIGIOUS EDUCATION CLASSES (TO DIFFERENT AGE-GROUPS)
From Johannes Lähnemann, *Nichtchristliche Religionen in Unterricht. Beiträge zu einer theologischen Didaktik der Weltreligionen. Schwerpunkt:*

Islam.[10] (Non-Christian Religions in the Classroom. Essays on a theological approach to the teaching of World Religions.)

I *Learning about World Religions in the Primary School*

    1 Pupils should show understanding for people of other confessions and religions; their behaviour towards pupils of other faiths should be without arrogance, fear or prejudice.

    2 The reasons for the unfamiliar patterns of behaviour of children and adults of other faiths should be explained to pupils in simple terms.

In this way, learning about other confessions/religions contributes to the overall aims of the primary school: that pupils should learn to live together in school where children come together with quite different backgrounds, and in which the less able require particular support.

II *Islam as a theme for the 'Common Course' in Secondary School (Years 1 and 2)*

The aims laid down the primary school are equally valid for the 'Common Course'. In particular, the first aim is again appropriate here: pupils should show understanding, interest, and behave naturally with people of other faiths. With increased capacity and readiness to learn, especially about things beyond pupils' own environment, the content of courses about other religions in the first and second years of secondary school can be extended considerably.

    1 Pupils should know that there are other important religions, apart from Christianity, in which many millions of people practise their faith devoutly.

    2 Islam should provide them with the example of the rise of an important non-Christian religion.

    3 They should be able to make simple comparisons between the beliefs and precepts of Christianity and Islam; they should be aware that testifying to the message of Christ does not exclude tolerance towards others.

    4 They should form an impression of the life of Muslims in the East.

    5 They should recognise the difficulties that people of other religions encounter in our (German) society, be aware of prejudices, and think of possible ways of overcoming them.

    6 They should behave naturally towards Muslim pupils, without arrogance, fear or prejudice (see aims for the primary school, above) and identify possibilities for actually meeting people of other faiths.

In this way, a closer study of Islam can help, on the one hand with the attainment of the aim of social integration appropriate to the 'Common Course', and on the other, to develop a more discriminating view of the world, as well as an awareness of the historical dimension.

III *Islam (and Hinduism)*

Secondary Stage I (Years 3–6)

    1 Pupils should become familiar with the ways of life and beliefs of Islam and Hinduism. They should become aware that these developed under particular historical, religious and social conditions,

and must be seen in the light of the fundamental issues and experiences of believers.

2 This insight will help them to be aware of existing prejudices towards these religions, to question them critically, and to arrive at a better understanding.

3 They should compare the means of salvation in these religions with those of Christianity, and establish the special nature of Christian redemption (self-sacrifice of God, forgiveness of sins, respect for others).

4 They should be able to appreciate the conflict in Islam and Hinduism between tradition and progress, and the attempts to overcome this conflict.

5 They should realise the necessity of overcoming barriers between religious communities in view of the disastrous consequences of religious intolerance in the past and in our own time.

Aims specifically related to Islam:

6 Pupils should gain insight into the historical dimension of Christianity and Islam as 'neighbours', both in war and in cultural cross-fertilisation.

7 They should appreciate the particular problems Muslims have in Germany, and above all the difficulties young people encounter in finding their role in society; they should behave sensitively towards them, but also be prepared to protect their social religious and cultural interests.

IV *Understanding the Purpose and Claims of Religions*
Secondary Stage II (Years 7–9)

Three aims are listed below which are specifically oriented towards the learning needs and requirements of Secondary Stage II; these should form a focus for the study of world religions.

1 Using selected examples, pupils should be able to compare critically the manifestations and comprehensibility of non-Christian religions with those of Christianity (in particular, the relationship between their origins and present-day religious, cultural, political and social contexts), but they should also be able to assess objectively the limits to understanding other religions.

2 In particular, they should have an appreciation of the fundamental experiences and patterns of life of other religions, and include them in a discussion of equivalent experiences in Christianity; they should use these to question the nature and form of their own existence.

3 They should be able to form a considered view concerning the obligation for the future of religions and philosophies (co-operation towards a world community living in harmony), and accept a personal involvement.

Appendix C

AN OUTLINE FOR AN ADVANCED COURSE OF TEACHER TRAINING IN THE PEDAGOGY OF 'FOREIGN' CHILDREN FOR GERMAN AND 'FOREIGN' TEACHERS

Ein Aufbaustudiengang 'Ausländerpädagogik' (mit dem Schwerpunkt der Ausbildung türkischer und deutscher Lehrer), wie er vom Verfasser geplant wird, soll ein breiteres Kernangebot gemeinsamer Studienelemente enthalten, während zusätzliche Angebote je für die deutschen und die türkischen Lehrer auf deren spezifische Defizite bezogen sind. Die folgende Auflistung hat sich aus der Erörterung von Konturen eines solchen Studienganges mit Fachkollegen aus der Lehrerausbildung ergeben:

I *Kernangebot für türkische und deutsche Lehrer*

	Mögliche Beteiligung folgender Fächer:
1 Einführung in türkisch/deutsche und islamisch/christliche Geschichte und Kultur sowie in die gegenwärtigen politischen und wirtschaftlichen Strukturen beider Länder	Geschichte Theologie/Religionswissenschaft Geographie Politologie
2 Sozialisationsprobleme türkischer Familien und Gruppen in der Bundesrepublik Deutschland/West Berlin (Minoritätenproblematik, Enkulturationsphänomene, Probleme des Bilinguismus . . .)	Sozialpädagogik Psychologie
3 Verfahren zur Förderung eines bilingualen Spracherwerbs (kontrastive Grammatik . . .)	Deutsch
4 Beteiligung an der Entwicklung (und Erprobung) von Curricula/Unterrichts-entwürfen in den beteiligten Schulfächern und für den zusätzlichen bilingualen/bikulturellen Unterricht	s. zu 1–3
5 Praktika im zusätzl. bilingualen/bikulturellen Unterricht, aber auch in Schulklassen mit Anteilen türkischer Kinder	

II *Spezifische Angebote für türkische Lehrer*

| 1 Sprachkurse (als Zugangsvoraussetzung zum Studium) | Goethe-Institute |
| 2 Einführung in Probleme des Spracherwerbs türkischer Schüler und der sprachlichen Kommunikation turkischer Schüler | Deutsch |

in ihrer Umgebung (Medien,
Freizeitverhalten . . .)
(soweit nicht bereits unter II, 1
angeboten)

3 Struktur des deutschen Schulwesens,   allgem, Pädagogik
Einführung in allgemeine deutsche   Schulpädagogik
Pädagogik, insbes. schulpädagogische   vergl. Pädagogik
Konzepte und Arbeitsweisen

III *Spezifische Angebote für deutsche Lehrer*
1 Einführung in die türkische Sprache   Lektoren für Turkisch
2 Lebensverhältnisse in der Türkei:
Leben im Familienverband,
Sippenstrukturen, Bräuche,
Rollenverhalten, Probleme der
ländlichen Strukturen, der
Urbanisierung

References

1 RAZVI, M. (1983) 'Was sollten muslimische Kinder über das Christentum wissen?', in LÄHNEMANN, J. (ed.) *Kulturbegegnung in Schule und Studium.* Hamburg-Rissen (1.3, 34–9, 35).

2 TWORUSCHKA, U. (1983) 'Perspektiven einer neuen Islam-Didaktik – vor dem Hintergrund bisheriger Behandlung des Islam in Schulbüchern und Unterrichtsmodellen', in LÄHNEMANN, J. (ed.) *Kulturbegegnung in Schule and Studium.* Hamburg-Rissen (1.4, 39–55, 41 ff.)

3 WEBER, W. (1981) *Christlich-islamische Begegnung: Eine mirchengemeinde und ihre türkischen Mitbürger.* Materialdienst der Ev. Zentralstelle für Weltanschauungsfragen. Stuttgart (340–9).

4 RAZVI, M. (1982) *Cultural Values and Education in a Multicultural Society – A Muslim View.* Strasbourg: Council of Europe (January 1982, 6–9, 8).

5 WOLFSON, H. A. (1956) 'The Muslim Attributes and the Christian Trinity', *Harvard Theological Review,* XLIX, 1–18.

6 *Learning for Living,* January 1972, 40–3, 40.

7 (1970) Newcastle upon Tyne: Oriel Press.

8 LÄHNEMANN, J. (1977) *Nichtchristliche Religionen im Unterricht.* (Trans. PROWSE, M. J. *Non-Christian Religions in the Classroom.*) Gütersloh: Mohn.

9 (1982) *NorthRhine-Westphalia Guidelines* (trans. PROWSE, M. J.). Neuss.

10 (1977) Gütersloh: Mohn (see 8, above).

Concluding Remarks

Stewart Sutherland

Editor's note Professor Sutherland's comments relate principally to the Consultation in which the preceding papers had their origin. As Conference Assessor it was his duty to select and comment on the most important points which were raised in discussion. The substance of his contribution at the time is found below.

The title 'Conference Assessor' which is assigned to me in the programme brings its own uncertainties. One might be representative of a firm of educational travel agents looking for suitable 'child-centred' locations for vacation-bound teachers worn out by a year in subject-centred schools. Or one might be a theological Egon Ronay spy looking for the strong meat of intellectual sustenance and aiming to expose the mushy peas of over-cooked piety. In this case one would have to point to the absence of any Asian flavour from the theological menu – an absence which impoverished it. However I shall avoid these pictures of my task and offer simply some concluding reactions and reflections.

The first comment must remind us that the title of the Conference is 'Theology and Education'. Inevitably – in the British context at least – the tendency was to assume implicitly that this meant 'Theology and Religious Education'. In one sense it does, but in Britain at least there is another much more confined sense of 'religious education' in which the latter is only one element within a broader educational context. This is the central sense given to 'religious education' here and its relationship to theology is a very well-ploughed field. We were partially successful in avoiding the assimilation of the debate about theology and education to the ongoing British discussion of religious education.

The second point to be made about the conference's understanding of the title is that almost without exception we understood it to be 'Christian Theology and Education'. In fact this was probably wise in view of our common interests and expertise, but it is as well to be clear that this was the working presumption of the discussion. Granted that this was so, the three obvious questions which dominated most of what was said from the platform and in discussion were:

1 What is theology?
2 What is education?
3 What is the relation between the two?

Not surprisingly the answers to the first two were rather varied and therefore there is no agreed 'composite' motion on the third which can summarise our findings.

There have been three expressions which have borne the weight of considerable accummulations of words in our discussions – 'critical openness', 'identity' and 'spirituality'. That we should have focused on these terms shows that we have been concerned to go to the heart of the matter. It would, however, be rather parsimonious simply to rehearse the differences in view over the meanings and relations between these expressions and I propose rather to reflect upon these differences, and to suggest that we must see them in a rather wider intellectual and cultural context.

The discussion between Professor Nipkow and Dr Hull on 'Can Theology have an Educational Role?' was bound to be very near, perhaps even at the heart of, our deliberations, and I wish to use the question set there about the role of theology *vis-à-vis* education as my starting point.

The main point which I wish to make is that the role of theology is to be an example, perhaps the last extant paradigm, of the problems which face us about the nature of education within our society. Theology is not in a fit state to provide the solution to our problems about the nature of education and the possibility of a spiritual or transcendent dimension to it. Rather theology shows, writ large, what those problems are. The possibility of achieving identity or integration through and in education is a problem which can be explored by finding analogies with the current state of theological discussion, rather than one to be solved by importing theological insights or premises.

To illustrate my point I return to another expression much used in this conference, and quite properly placed at the centre of our discussion by Professor Hirst. The problems in question are those associated with and deriving from the extension within the Western world (once called 'Christendom'!) of the methods of critical-openness to matters constitutive of and matters approximate to religious faith.

It would be a mistake, of course, to see this as an invention or product of the twentieth century. At one level one could argue that a major responsibility lies with Erasmus. Little did he realise – one suspects – where it would lead, when he set out to prepare the best critical text of the New Testament which he could. This scholarly ambition hid some dramatic and fundamental presuppositions; the most crucial of these was that one could transfer the scholarly critical apparatus used to reconstruct the texts of Greek philosophy and literature, without change, to interrogate the existing Holy Scriptures of the Christian religion. The enquiring mind of the historian and linguist were released upon the preserves of faith. Problems were set then with which the churches are still wrestling. Of course, I over-simplify and over-dramatise, but the point stands.

Perhaps it is appropriate, while marking the 75th anniversary of Westhill College, to refer to the Reformation, albeit through a historically distorted lens. I want to quote two short passages from John Osborne's play *Luther*.[1] The historical analysis of this play, presented with devastating wit by Professor Gordon Rupp,[2] does not invalidate the point that the critical techniques of Erasmus were connected with all the subtleties of the web of history to the critical rejection of human religious authority to be found in Luther. In Osborne's reconstruction of the Diet of Worms, Eck's closing questions to Luther are as follows:

> Do reasons have to be given to anyone who cares to ask a question? Any question? Why, if anyone who questioned the common understanding of the Church on any matter he liked to raise, and had to be answered irrefutably from the Scriptures, there would be nothing certain or decided in Christendom. What would the Jews and Turks and Saracens say if they heard us *debating* whether what we have always believed is true or not?

The words of this concluding scene in Act Two are followed at the opening of the third and final Act by the words spoken by the symbolic figure of the Knight, in Wittenberg four years later (1525):

> There was excitement that day. In Worms – that day I mean. Oh, I don't mean now, not now. A lot's happened since then. There's no excitement like that any more. Not unless murder's your idea of excitement. I tell you, you can't have ever known the kind of thrill that monk set off amongst that collection of all kinds of men gathered together there – those few years ago. We all felt it, every one of us, just without any exception, you couldn't help it, even if you didn't want to, and, believe me, most of those people didn't want to. His scalp looked blotchy and itchy, and you felt sure, just looking at him, his body must be permanently sour and white all over, even whiter than his face and like a millstone to touch. He'd sweated so much by the time he'd finished, I could smell every inch of him even from where I was. But he fizzed like a hot spark in a trail of gunpowder going off in us, that dowdy monk, he went off in us, and nothing could stop it, and it blew up and there was nothing we could do, any of us, that was it. I just felt quite sure, quite certain in my own mind nothing could ever be the same again, just simply that.

Osborne may have been over-influenced by the psychoanalytic account of Luther by Erik Erikson,[3] but there is dramatic truth in his presentation of the consequences for social relationships of what we call 'critical openness'. It is significant that Luther the reformer is also Luther the scholar who exemplifies in his own writings the constraints of the tensions between critical openness in intellectual matters and the search for depth and integrity in the life of faith – a tension which threatens to rend both theology and the church today.

What I refer to is the gap between critical scholarship and the life of the church at local level. It is no exaggeration to say that what are accepted by theologians as intellectual commonplaces simply have not been absorbed into the intellectual and theological bloodstream of the churches. A number of those parish priests who are theologically aware have told me that they could not possibly go into the pulpit on a Sunday and expound the beliefs which they *as Christians* hold. Whether they are to be pitied or commended is not my point; such attitudes are symptomatic of the problems of theology. I do not therefore find the distinction made between 'sitting' and 'kneeling' theology a helpful one. This restates rather than solves the problem to which I am pointing. To import such distinctions into education from theology can only distract us from the necessity of redefining the issues at stake.

To some this will seem to be unduly pessimistic and it does raise the question of whether there is more to be said about theology. I believe that there is much more to be said, but that in order to make progress we must see that the problems besetting both theology and education belong to a much wider context. The first move must be to extend our metaphors from 'sitting' and 'kneeling' to 'holding at arm's length'. Much of what goes on in theology and in education involves holding at arm's length what is most naturally and appropriately held in embrace. The beliefs and values which we hold out for scrutiny lest they be the products of blindness or prejudice are, again most naturally, matters of deep-seated conviction which involve emotion as well as intellect, soul as well as mind.

Critical openness, central as it is to our Western culture, both liberates and causes problems. We have all experienced the fruits of liberation in the quality of our lives, but the problems also belong there, and they arise because critical openness requires the mastery of a very difficult technique – that of distancing oneself from what is nearest to one and in that sense primary. This distancing requires one to objectify that which most fully belongs to one's subjectivity. One has to hold at arm's length both what is personal or individual and partly experienced in that sense, and also what is experiential in the different sense of belonging to the communal and 'institutional' world of ritual.

As we were reminded by Monsignor Nichols earlier in the conference, Newman referred to intellectuals as 'not normally devout', and in part this reflects the capacity of such intellectuals to live at arm's length from much of what is experiential, particularly in the second sense outlined above. However, although such intellectuals have always been with us, through the expansion of education, the critical openness which is the breeding ground of such detachment has a much wider constituency. It has not produced an extended class of intellectuals in Newman's sense, but rather the legacy of a very large portion of our population for whom in certain selected areas of life questioning comes more naturally than affirming. By and large, these areas include religion.

Now these are very sweeping claims and the analysis lying behind them does not belong to the present context. However, by way of making them a little more plausible and accessible, I will point to three symptoms of my diagnosis of the situation.

The first may seem, but is not, *completely* frivolous, and is the heartfelt cry of one who occasionally chairs university committees. The basic skills and brilliance of academics are those appropriate to the principles of falsification – or, more bluntly, picking holes in arguments! This can be both dazzling and bewitching unless decisions and therefore affirmations are urgently required, yet it is the distillation of critical openness taken to its finest resolution.

More generally, the rise of the cult figure of the journalist earlier in the century, and of the television interviewer at the present time, is at its worst – and with notable exceptions – based on the type of scepticism which parasitically awaits the affirmations of others for verbal dissection.

Or again, the increasing importance of views for which no individual takes responsibility, in both political and public life, is very marked. Opinion polls and surveys affect political decisions, voting patterns, the packaging and sales of goods and so on, in a way which shows quite clearly that such detachment of opinions from individuals is a force within rather than a reflection of our way of life. Kierkegaard caught the point beautifully when he defined 'the public' as 'that curious entity formed by everyone becoming a third party'.

Of course, these impressionistic comments do not prove my analysis to be true but I do hope they make clearer my claim about the variety of ways in which 'critical openness' has entered into the very fabric of our lives, sometimes to liberate, but sometimes, by the objectification or distancing necessary to it, to cause difficulties for us.

The difficulties to which I have pointed in these commonplace examples are relatively superficial, but in more significant controls and in the hands of others they are shown to be very profound indeed. This is the point to which I have been leading. Theologians and educationists are not alone in facing these problems, and it is a form of tunnel vision to believe that they are. The same culture to which we belong, and which is moulded by the tentacles of critical openness having extended far through religious belief and educational practice, has nurtured those who have diagnosed the problems from different perspectives. Our culture is rich in resources upon which theologians and educators must draw. I think primarily now of literature, and I can exemplify only by reminding myself of the names of some of those novelists who have much to teach us about the distancing which follows such openness – Dostoevsky, Lawrence, Achebe (*Things Fall Apart*), Saul Bellow, Raymond Williams (*Border Country*), Lewis Grassic Gibbon (*Scots Quair*), or Edmund Gosse (*Father and Son*).

The lessons which arise from this for those who will reflect further on theology and education are four in number.

The first in that the discussion will be unfruitful if we set up a gladiatorial contest between theologians and educationists to decide which presupposition will dominate the other. The context of the discussion is much broader, for the ills which afflict both theology and education belong to our whole culture.

The second point is that theologians must learn from the dialogue with educationists that major problems have been set for theologians and churchmen by the universality in our culture of a compulsory educational system which rightly retains critical openness as one of its premises. The need for proper theological education of believers, lay and clerical is desperately urgent, and as this conference has made plain Britain has much to learn from both Germany and the United States of America on this matter.

Third, equally the educationist must learn from the theology and from the religious communities. Theologians and believers have the great merit that they have kept the central questions in this area alive. These questions concern the nature (or doctrine) of man, and also the question of how far critical openness is sufficient as the single foundation for education, let alone society. The danger of that as a single foundation is, as I have hinted, that it lends undue weight to the over- or even complete objectification of human life and values. The point is perhaps best and most briefly made if we reflect on the fact that the theologians have never sold out to behaviourism. Theologians, because of the very nature of theology, have never denied the profound distinction between human beings and machines, although practitioners of every branch of the physical, biological and social sciences certainly have. Educationists who must enter into dialogue with these sciences have in some cases been seduced by the elements of them which lead towards the behaviouristic premises which would reduce education to indoctrination. A continuing engagement with theology might serve appropriately as the intellectual chastity belt which interrupts the progress of the seducer!

The final point is to remind theologians and educationists of those pockets of light which still illuminate with clarity and precision our intellectual landscape – to be found in the art of some novelists in particular, and in the humanities in general.

References

1 OSBORNE, JOHN (1961) *Luther.* London: Faber and Faber.
2 RUPP, E. GORDON (1961–2) 'John Osborne and the historical Luther', *Expository Times,* 73, 147 ff.
3 ERIKSON, ERIK H. (1959) *Young Man Luther.* London: Faber and Faber.

Index of Subjects

Advent, 63
aesthetic experience, 64, 111–13
affections, 6, 20, 81, 89
affiliative experience, 64
AFFOR, 93, 100
Agreed Syllabus, 49, 54, 86, 115
Allah, 126, 127, 132
America, *see* United States
Anglican Church, 44, 61, 62, 77–9
anthropology, 86
apologetics, 89
apostolic, 65
assent, 19–21
assembly, 81, 128
attitudes, 5, 6, 13, 32, 58, 64, 81, 89
authority, 9, 31, 64–5, 76, 88
autonomy, 9, 19, 24, 33, 42, 57, 83, 86
  of religious education, 47

baptism, 60–3, 66, 70, 77, 79
belief, 6–11, 13, 32, 51, 63
belonging, 33
behaviourism, 142
Bible, *see* scripture
Britain, *see* United Kingdom
British Council of Churches, 56, 75, 76
Buddhism, 59, 89, 114

catechesis, 7, 9, 14, 17–19, 43–4, 47, 56–75, 78
Christianity, Christendom, 1, 13, 14, 26, 40–1, 45–7, 67, 76, 90, 119, 126–7, 129, 133–4, 138–9
cognition, 5–7, 12, 20–1, 25–6, 32, 101, 111, 112
colleges, 45, 81, 99, 129
commitment, 2, 3, 7, 8, 13–14, 20–1, 34, 35, 53, 57, 62, 67, 74, 76, 80, 82, 88, 91, 97, 102, 115, 117
community, 2, 60, 64–6, 68–9, 72–5, 77, 93, 117, 125, 128
conceptualisation, forms of, 10, 11, 43
confession, 31–2, 34, 47, 123, 126, 128, 133
confirmation, 32, 77
constitution, 1, 24, 35
contemplation, 65–6, 69, 93
convergence, 28, 42, 43, 94
conversion, 2, 21, 62–3, 66, 69
creeds, 68, 72
critical openness, *see* openness
culture, 3, 51–2, 57–8, 66, 68, 112, 116, 119, 122–3, 127–30, 134, 138, 141–2
curriculum, 41, 49, 70–1, 81–7, 130

death, 118
democracy, 84, 122
demythologising, 34, 99
denomination, 64, 71, 83
dialogue, 1, 2, 14, 21, 30, 35, 74, 83, 90–1, 123, 125, 131, 141–2
dimensions, 110
  of life, 117
  of religion, 94
differentiation, 30, 32
dissociation, 31, 34
diversity, 2, 5, 7, 13, 57, 75, 89, 91, 97, 110
doctrine, 20, 25, 27, 124
  of man, 82

Easter, 63
ecumenical movement, 35, 97
education, 1–3, 6–7, 9, 12, 18–19, 45, 58, 71, 82, 97, 98, 101, 108, 113–21, 125, 128, 137–8, 140–1

143

Index of Names